EXPLORI
THE HISTORY OF MEDICINE

From the Ancient Physicians of Pharaoh to Genetic Engineering

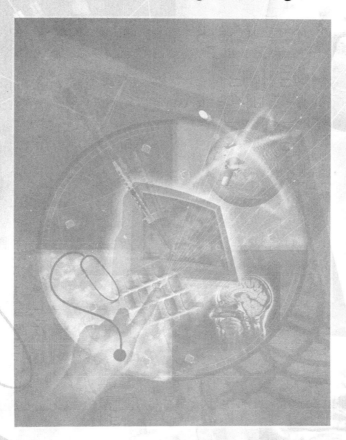

JOHN HUDSON TINER

Master Books

EXPLORING
THE HISTORY OF MEDICINE

First printing: April 1999
Seventh printing: October 2007

For information write: Master Books,
P.O. Box 726, Green Forest, AR 72638

ISBN-13: 978-0-89051-248-7
ISBN-10: 0-89051-248-5
Library of Congress: 99-70076

Interior Design by Brent Spurlock

Cover Design by Left Coast Design, Portland, Oregon.

Printed in the United States of America.

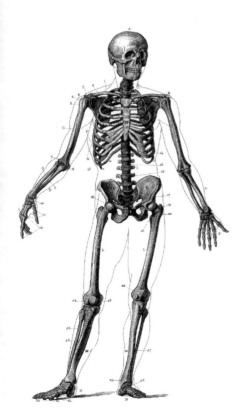

Dedication
*This book is dedicated to
Samuel Conner Stephens*

Master
Books
A Division of New Leaf Publishing Group

Table of Contents

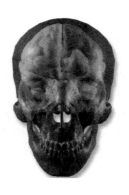

The First Physicians

Do you know the name of the most ancient doctor known? The physician Imhotep (pronounced im-HOH-tep) lived 55 centuries ago, in 3500 B.C., in Egypt. He earned fame in many fields — as a politician, astronomer, architect, and physician. He designed the first pyramid — an elaborate tomb for one of the Egyptian pharaohs.

Ancient Egyptian physicians worked harder at keeping the body free of decay after death than at keeping it free of disease during life. They believed the road to eternal life lay in preserving the body. They developed an effective way to embalm bodies. Some Egyptian mummies are still around today.

In addition to preparing bodies for burial, Imhotep may have performed simple surgical operations. But any break-

SYMPTOMS

1. Doctors relied on myths and magical powers.

2. Some doctors were mistreating their patients.

3. Doctors did not understand how the body worked.

Can You Diagnose the Discoveries?

The first physicians known to western medicine were located in Egypt, Greece, and Rome.

Imhotep is considered the first known physician. He is shown below in a re-creation of an Egyptian wall painting. The primary duty of an Egyptian doctor was to prepare bodies for the afterlife.

throughs in medicine that he may have made are buried in the mists of time. We know his name and little else.

A more famous ancient physician is Hippocrates (pronounced hi-POK-ruh-teez). We not only know his name, but also know other facts about his life and his medical discoveries. Plato, one of the best-known Greek philosophers, mentioned Hippocrates by name, as did Aristotle, another Greek scientist. They thought well of him and considered him the greatest doctor of their day.

Hippocrates, a Greek, was born in 460 B.C., almost 2,500 years ago, on the island of Kos. This rocky little island is north of Rhodes off the coast of Asia Minor.

Although he lived so long ago, we do have a good idea of what he looked like. In 1933, workers uncovered on Kos a statue of Hippocrates. The statue shows him as a short man, rather stately in his robe, with a bold, courageous look to his face.

He needed all the boldness he could muster to change how doctors practiced medicine.

Other doctors based their healing art upon the belief that evil spirits, hateful demons, and vengeful gods struck people with diseases. Invisible arrows shot by the Greek god Apollo caused pain. One treatment for disease called for the victim to travel to one of the many pagan temples in Greece. The sick person made a sacrifice and then spent the night in the temple. As he slept, he was supposed to dream away the sickness.

Hippocrates visited Egypt early in life and studied medicine there. He taught at various places, including Athens. Eventually he returned home and began a school of medicine on Kos.

Hippocrates taught methods that must have seemed strange to doctors who expected to treat their patients with chanting and magic potions. Hippocrates changed all of that. He believed every disease had a natural cause. "Find the cause," he said, "then you can cure the disease."

He perfected what today would be called a good bedside manner. He gained the confidence of patients and put their minds at ease. Hippocrates instructed his students to find out as much as possible about the patient. "Ask the patient about the symptoms. How did he feel when the illness began? Question him about what he usually eats and drinks. Did he change his diet?"

"Allow the patient to rest," he advised. "See that he is kept clean, has fresh air and simple wholesome food." This was good advice because doctors knew so little about medicine. God has given the body the ability to heal itself if given time to work.

Older doctors couldn't abide by the new ways. They expected patients to make sacrifices to Greek gods and goddesses at the many pagan temples. "The gods will be angry," these doctors warned. "They will punish doctors and patients who dare to defy them."

We know in detail what Hippocrates taught because his students made careful notes of his lectures. They collected the notes and published books in his name. More than 50 books carrying his name have come down to us.

For instance, Hippocrates said,

Hippocrates is known as the "Father of Medicine." He is considered one of the greatest physicians the world has ever known.

"Desperate diseases require desperate remedies," and, "Illness is sometimes stronger when a mind is troubled."

His study of diet also convinced him that "one man's meat is another man's poison." In other words, the same food can make one person sick but cause no harm to another person.

Hippocrates also made changes in how physicians looked upon their profession. During his time, a doctor was

This Scamnum was a medical instrument used by Hippocrates.

Hippocrates is refusing the bribes of a rich man who wants him to make a person sick on purpose. This is one of the reasons that he developed the Hippocratic Oath. His oath is still taken by doctors today.

sometimes bribed to see that a patient died, or asked to prepare poison to kill an enemy. Suppose a ruler wanted to rid himself of a rival. He could hire a court physician who would see that the rival became sick and died.

Hippocrates taught against such improper conduct. He told his students to treat everyone the same — both friends and foes, rich and poor. "Sometimes give your services for nothing," he urged his students. "For where there is love of man, there is also love of medicine."

He drew up a statement describing proper conduct. The pledge, called the Hippocratic Oath, is a guideline for honorable standards of action. Medical students still take it upon completion of their course of training. The statement says in part, "I will use treatment to help the sick according to my ability and judgment, but never with the view to injury and wrong doing . . . Into whatsoever houses I enter, I will enter to help the sick."

Hippocrates, the remarkable physician of Kos, is still, even today, considered one of the greatest physicians the world has ever known. His advice to doctors is still being taught in medical schools. He is rightly called the "Father of Medicine."

Galen's ideas about medicine were held in such high regard that his books were used by doctors for hundreds of years.

The Golden Age of Greece ended when the Romans conquered most of the civilized world.

Roman medicine aimed at helping society as a whole, rather than individuals. They built aqueducts to carry fresh water, arranged for sewers to carry away waste, and built public baths for personal cleanliness.

The most important physician during the Roman Empire was Galen, a Greek. A thorough knowledge of the body is essential to good medical practice. Galen believed that "a physician needs to study the body, as an architect needs to follow a plan."

The Romans had passed harsh laws against dissecting human bodies. A doctor who dared open a body merely to satisfy his curiosity risked severe punishment. Galen dared not break the laws.

Galen traveled to Alexandria to study medicine. Alexandria was a Greek city established in Egypt by Alexander the Great. It was a Roman city in Galen's time. Alexandria boasted a teaching museum and huge library, the best in the world. It was the nearest thing to a modern university.

At Alexandria, Galen could study two complete human skeletons. Later, he dissected animals — pigs, goats, and even apes. He described what he saw in careful detail. He learned a lot from his study of animals, but not everything he learned about animals could be used to treat humans.

Galen returned to his hometown, Pergamum. There he served as physician at a school for gladiators. Although the Romans forbade dissection of dead bodies, they encouraged professional warriors to hack themselves apart for the amusement of coliseum crowds. Once the warrior died, his body could not be touched except to prepare it for burial.

Galen repaired the injured fighters and learned firsthand about the human body.

After three years, Galen traveled to Rome. He studied some more and wrote the first of his many books. He also took on his first important case. Eudemus, a well-known physician, suffered a mild paralysis in his right hand. He could not move his third and fourth fingers. The best physicians in the city examined him. All of them failed to restore feeling to his fingers.

As a last resort, Eudemus sent for Galen, the new doctor in town.

Galen examined the fingers. Then he asked, "Did you injure your back or neck or strike your head recently?"

Puzzled, Eudemus answered, "Yes. I

Galen became one of the most famous doctors in Rome. He is shown on the left in this picture experimenting in the mixing of medicine.

was thrown from a chariot. I struck my neck against a stone. I recovered from the fall."

"Not entirely," Galen said. "Nerves from the fingers connect to the spinal column in the neck. Your neck injury caused the numbness in your hand."

Galen treated the nerve in Eudemus' neck and not his fingers. Feeling came back. Before long, Eudemus could move his fingers again. He recovered completely.

Galen's fame soared. So did the jealousy of the other doctors. He didn't endear himself to them by being very sure of himself. He was the best doctor in the empire. He knew it and made sure everyone else knew it, too.

Marcus Aurelius, the emperor, hired Galen as his personal physician. The emperor summed up his opinion of his personal physician by saying, "Rome has but one physician — Galen."

Christians lived in Rome and in Pergamum, too. Pergamum was home to one of the "seven churches of Asia" mentioned in Revelation (Rev. 1:11). Although Galen himself never became a Christian, he believed in one God, the creator of all things. He believed the Creator designed every part of the human body for a particular purpose.

According to Galen, the existence of God the Creator could not be dismissed once a person saw the marvelous complexity of the human body. He said, "Every man who looks at things with an open mind, seeing a spirit living in this mass of flesh and humors, and examining the structure of any animal whatever . . . will comprehend the excellence of the Spirit which is in heaven."

As the end of his life drew to a close,

Galen visited his home town, Pergamum, once again. He died there in A.D. 200. His fame continued to grow.

His ideas didn't die with him. He had written a huge number of books — about 125 — of which 80 still exist. His books contain a curious mixture of fact, opinion, and outright errors. With his usual cheerful self-confidence, Galen stated it all as fact. He did not keep apart what he knew as fact from what he merely believed to be true.

Galen's effect upon medicine grew, rather than became less, with time. His views came to be regarded as the final authority in medicine. During the Middle Ages in Europe, scholars avoided experimentation and direct experience. Instead, they simply looked for answers in Galen's books. His dead hand held medicine in its grip with a firmness never matched before or since.

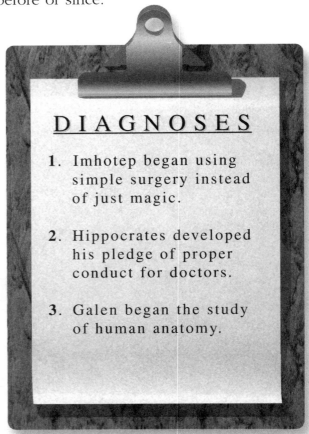

DIAGNOSES

1. Imhotep began using simple surgery instead of just magic.

2. Hippocrates developed his pledge of proper conduct for doctors.

3. Galen began the study of human anatomy.

Answer T or F for true or false, or
Select A or B for the phrase that best completes the sentence.

T F   1. The medical discoveries of the Egyptian doctor Imhotep are well-known today.

A B   2. The most famous ancient Greek doctor was (A. Plato; B. Hippocrates).

T F   3. One of the Greek treatments for disease was to have the sick person dream away the sickness in a pagan temple.

A B   4. Older doctors predicted that doctors who followed Hippocrates' teaching would be (A. punished; B. rewarded) by the gods and goddesses.

A B   5. The Hippocratic Oath for doctors is (A. a pledge of proper conduct; B. a schedule of prices a doctor should charge).

A B   6. The title given to Hippocrates is (A. Father of Greek Philosophy; B. Father of Medicine).

A B   7. The most important physician during Roman times was (A. Galen; B. Socrates).

A B   8. The city of Alexandria was noted for its huge (A. aqueduct; B. library).

A B   9. Galen learned firsthand about the human body from (A. dissecting the bodies of criminals; B. treating injured gladiators).

T F   10. When Galen went to Rome he was put in prison.

T F   11. Galen believed that the marvelous complexity of the human body pointed to a Creator.

Greek Medicine Goes Wrong

Beginning in A.D. 400, Roman rule weakened. Bickering among its leaders took its toll. After that, about A.D. 500, the Huns and Vandals overran the northern and western parts of the empire. They smashed the Roman Empire and left behind a number of small, weak countries ruled by quarreling kings. Later, the Arabs captured the southern and eastern part of the empire.

Darkness fell across Europe for a thousand years. Practically all interest in learning new facts ceased. Disease, unrest, and wars reduced Europe to a semi-barbaric state. Repeatedly the Black Death, or bubonic plague, swept across Europe. It killed as many as one person of every three. No one could guess its cause or cure it. The struggle for survival left little time for the luxury of studying books about medicine or any other scientific subject.

SYMPTOMS

1. It was illegal to study anatomy using humans.

2. Europe fell into the Dark Ages where new learning ceased.

Can You Diagnose the Discoveries?

During Greek and Roman times, people expected their leaders to be able to read and write. In Europe during the Dark Ages, this was not the case. Charlemagne (pronounced shahr-luh-MAIN), the most enlightened leader of the Dark Ages, learned to read only as an adult. He never learned to write.

One reason for this was that so many books had been destroyed. In Alexandria, a mob had burned the museum and library with its fabulous collection of books. The books, which had been gathered over a period of six hundred years, went up in smoke. Arab conquerors carried away the contents of other great libraries.

All the vast knowledge of Greece and Rome was found in the few books left in scattered libraries across Europe. Books became so special that people treated them with great respect. For that reason, books by ancient writers like Hippocrates and Galen took on special importance. Hippocrates and Galen, two of the first physicians, became the last word in medicine. Yet, their books contained many errors.

For instance, Galen believed disease resulted from an imbalance of the vital fluids, or humors, of the body. He said, "The body has in itself blood, phlegm, yellow bile, and black bile . . . We enjoy the most perfect health when these elements are in the right proportion."

Even today, a person in good health is said to be in "good humor," while a person feeling poorly is said to be in "ill humor."

If the four-humor view of disease were true, then curing disease would merely mean bringing the body fluids into balance. Doctors restored the balance by changing the diet or by bleeding the patient.

This practice of bloodletting continued throughout many centuries. It lasted into the 1800s. George Washington is probably the best-known victim of the four-humor theory of disease. He caught a cold one winter while riding his horse on his Mount Vernon farm. His doctors decided an excess of blood caused the cold. They opened his veins and drained

The doctor in this picture is trying to bring the body's vital fluids into balance by removing excess blood. This bloodletting procedure was based on false ideas as described by Galen in his book. When George Washington took a bad cold, his doctors bled him to death trying to remove his excess blood.

out some of his blood. When he didn't improve, they did it again. In the end, Washington's own doctors bled him to death. Their practice was based on Galen's books.

A knowledge of the human body is one of the most important things a doctor must know. Anatomy is the study of the human body. The word anatomy is a Greek word meaning "to cut." One way to study anatomy is to cut or dissect a dead body to examine its parts.

The Greeks regarded the human body as very special. They prided themselves upon physical perfection. They passed laws forbidding anyone from dissecting a body, even doctors.

How could any doctor learn about muscles, nerves, organs, and bones without seeing them?

Hippocrates did try to describe the whole body, although he could not see under the skin. He believed the heart to be the center of life. He considered the brain merely a cooling organ for the blood. Arteries were given their name because the word artery is a Greek word meaning "I carry air." Apparently, the Greeks did not even know that arteries carried blood.

Galen made the first attempts to master anatomy. He dissected animals — dogs, goats, pigs, and monkeys. He described what he saw in careful detail. He discovered that arteries carried blood and not air.

Not everything he saw in the animals held true in the human body. For example, he found a network of blood vessels below the brain in most of the animals he investigated, and he assumed those blood vessels were an important part of the human body also. Today we know that the blood vessels Galen described are common in animals, but they are not found in human beings.

Although Galen warned doctors to study firsthand for themselves, his advice went unheeded. Galen, the successful doctor, stated his views with force and confidence. Doctors who followed him frowned upon independent study.

Medical schools used Galen's books as textbooks for more than a thousand years. He became the undisputed authority. No one dared to ever differ with him.

Galen performs a surgical procedure on a live pig in this picture published in 1586. He applied what he learned from animal anatomy to his study of the human body.

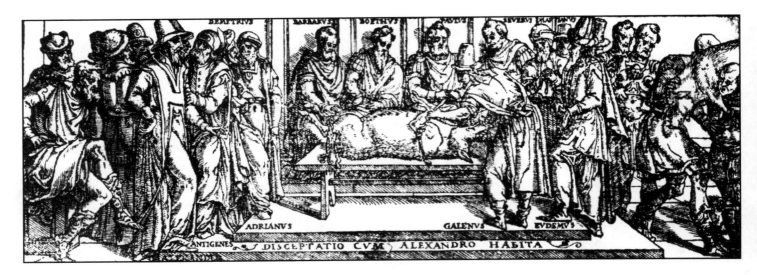

OCRISIS PRAECOGNITIO C

IVSTVS   GALENVS

BAMANTIS DIGNOTIO

A physician is taking a women's pulse in this illustration from one of Galen's books published in 1588. Galen's writings were part of the reason that medicine advanced so slowly during the middle ages. Every word was taught as fact without question.

The Various Roles of a Physician from 1588 was one of the many books written about Hippocrates. His students took notes on his teachings and published over 50 books about his ideas, many of which are still being used today.

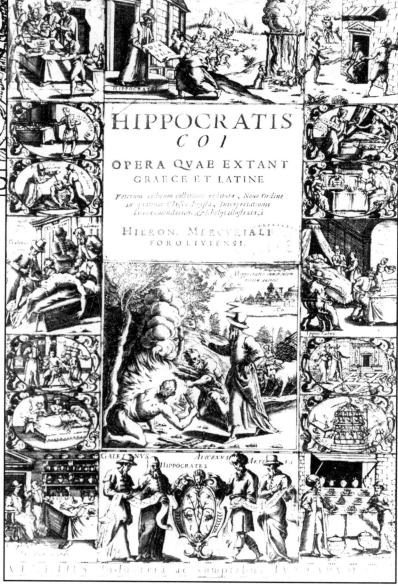

Let's look at a medical school of the 1500s and see how medicine was taught. Jacobus Sylvius taught at the University of Paris. He was one of the best-known doctors of his day. As many as 400 students attended his medical classes.

Jacobus Sylvius enters the lecture hall. He walks up a little flight of steps to his chair on a raised platform. He sits down in a chair and arranges a well-worn book — one of Galen's — on the reading desk before him. He opens the book and begins reading. Students hastily scribble notes.

Jacobus Sylvius is the typical surgeon of the Middle Ages. He relied on Galen and Hippocrates' books more than what he observed with his own eyes.

Galen taught that the liver was five-lobed, that the breastbone had seven segments, that a network of blood vessels could be found under the brain. Sylvius believes every word of it, although those features couldn't be found in the body right under his eyes. He saw exactly what Galen told him he would see!

If the corpse and book don't agree, then the error is in the corpse! No one would dream of doubting Galen.

Yet, someone will soon dream of doing just that. During Sylvius' own lifetime, the grip of Galen's dead hand upon medicine will begin to weaken. It won't happen without a fight.

Usually animals like sheep or pigs are dissected to illustrate the lecture. About once a year, Sylvius conducts a dissection of a human body. The corpse is usually that of a convicted criminal who has been hanged for his crimes. Like other doctors, Sylvius considers it beneath his dignity to cut the body himself. Instead, an assistant does the actual cutting of flesh. Another assistant points to each part as the professor reads aloud.

Often what Sylvius reads and the assistant points to don't agree. Sylvius steadfastly refuses to see any errors in Galen.

DIAGNOSES

1. Galen studied the anatomy of animals and applied it to humans.

2. Doctors relied on the teachings of Hippocrates and Galen for over a thousand years.

*Answer T or F for true or false, or
select A or B for the phrase that best completes the sentence.*

T F   1. Charlemagne was an important writer during the Dark Ages.

A B   2. Alexandria's great library was (A. preserved in Egypt; B. burned by a mob).

T F   3. The books by Hippocrates and Galen were free of errors.

T F   4. Doctors used bloodletting because they believed it put the body's four humors in balance.

T F   5. The treatment George Washington received was based on the four-humors theory of disease.

A B   6. Anatomy is the study of (A. the human body; B. stars and planets).

T F   7. Medical schools used Galen's books as the final word in medicine.

T F   8. Jacobus Sylvius taught medical students by reading from a book while an assistant carried out a dissection.

Fabric of the Body

Andreas Vesalius (pronounced veh-SAY-lee-us) was born just before midnight on December 31, 1514. His mother was English, his father Belgian. Andreas Vesalius came from a long line of doctors. Both his great-grandfather and grandfather were physicians. His father was a successful apothecary (druggist).

It became clear that Andreas wanted to follow the family profession. Vesalius' father encouraged him. He built his son a small laboratory where Andreas could experiment.

At the age of 17, Andreas Vesalius began medical studies at the University of Paris. He was a quick-thinking, confident young man. He soon tired of hearing Sylvius reading aloud hour after hour from old books. Medicine should be more than

SYMPTOMS

1. Human anatomy was difficult to study because of decay.

2. Medical professors were teaching ideas that were wrong.

3. Students accepted these ideas without experimenting to see if they were right.

Can You Diagnose the Discoveries?

a matter of saying "Galen said this," and "Galen said that." Why did professors teach things they'd never tried?

Because of his early reading and experimenting, Vesalius was much more advanced than other students — and even many of his teachers. He could hardly stand to watch the ignorant assistants make hasty, blundering dissections. "I would learn more facts from a butcher in his meat market!" he said.

Once, during a particularly bad dissection, Andreas Vesalius rose in disgust, strode to the table, and snatched up the scalpel. Skillfully he laid back the flesh and uncovered the missing organ.

Vesalius resolved that when he became a doctor he would personally conduct dissections. "There is only one book from which to learn about the human body," Vesalius said, "and that's the human body itself."

In 1536, life in Paris became difficult for foreign students. War had broken out, and Belgium was on the other side. Vesalius left Paris to study at the University of Louvain, near Brussels, Belgium.

While at Louvain he seized a chance to study the human body in more detail. Outside the city wall he found a skeleton of a robber left hanging on a gallows. Birds had picked the bones clean. Vesalius crept outside the city wall during the dead of night and cut down the skeleton. He smuggled it into the city a few bones at a time.

Andreas Vesalius was the first master of human anatomy. His careful studies provided doctors with the accurate information they needed to save lives.

Back in his room, he wired together the human skeleton. He studied it until he knew every bone, even while blindfolded.

Galen taught that the breastbone had seven segments. Yet the breastbone of this skeleton had only three parts. How could the teacher have made such a mistake?

Then Vesalius made a horrifying discovery. He compared an ape skeleton with his human skeleton. The ape's breastbone did have seven segments. Galen had gained his information from apes. Doctors treated humans based on descriptions of apes.

Later, in 1537, Vesalius traveled to Padua for further study. Padua University,

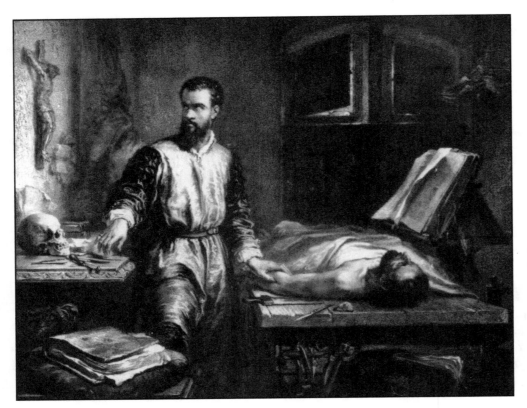

Vesalius is shown working on his study of human anatomy. He carefully compared what was in Galen's books to what he actually saw in the human body. He found several mistakes that his medical professors were teaching.

about 20 miles from Venice, was Europe's most famous school. Students ran the university. They hired their own teachers by popular vote. Because students paid the professors' salaries, they could demand the best. Professors who did poorly were asked to leave. Padua became the great scientific center of Vesalius' day. It attracted students from all over Europe.

On December 5, 1537, he earned his medical degree. Although only 22 years old, the medical faculty recognized his abilities. They elected him professor of anatomy the next day. As Vesalius had promised himself, he taught anatomy by conducting each dissection himself.

Other professors wondered why he wasted his time with messy, time-consuming dissections. "Galen has described the human body perfectly," these professors said. "Dissections serve no purpose. Students can learn anatomy just as well by reading a book."

Vesalius' lectures became immensely popular. As many as four hundred students crowded into the lecture hall. The popularity introduced a new problem. Most students could not see very well because of the crowd. Even a class of 20 students would be too large for everyone to see the smaller organs.

Also, the corpse could not be preserved. Within a few days, it began to decompose. Vesalius had to work quickly. Students had little time to observe and think about what they saw.

Vesalius overcame the problem by making illustrations. He drew huge charts showing the veins, arteries, and nervous system, and hung the charts in the classroom. Students could see at a glance what would take hours to explain. His drawings were instantly successful. Students copied the drawings by hand and passed the copies along to their friends.

Vesalius kept a copy of Galen's books on hand and marked changes in them. He found over two hundred mistakes in the ancient books — mistakes still being taught by doctors of his day.

He even found one mistake in his own teaching!

Galen had taught that a network of little blood vessels existed right under the brain. Vesalius always had trouble finding that particular feature in humans, although he could locate it without difficulty in animals. During dissections, he kept the head of a sheep on hand. If he failed to locate the network at the base of the human brain, he could show his students the elusive feature in the sheep instead.

One day Vesalius once again failed to find the network of little blood vessels. He thought back to all the other dissections. Why, he'd never seen the network in a human body. As it turned out, the network occurs in some animals, but not in human beings.

Now Vesalius could understand how doctors could see one thing but teach another. They had repeated Galen for so long it had blinded them to the true facts. He himself had even fallen into that trap. Incredible!

He decided to write a new book to correct all the errors he'd uncovered. He wanted his book to be useful. Instead of long descriptions, he would use line drawings so the essential points could be quickly grasped. He chose Jan Stephen van Calcar, a young artist, to make the drawings. This met immediate opposition by the doctors. What could an artist possibly teach a doctor?

Illustration of a human body, showing the major muscle groups, by Andreas Vesalius. This image was published in his landmark "De Humani Corporis Fabrica" (The fabric of the human body).

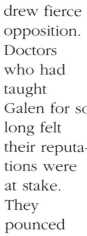

Actually, the artists of the 1500s knew far more about the human body than even the best doctors. Michelangelo and the other great artists studied the human body so they could paint it accurately. Medical students could learn more about the muscles of the human body from Michelangelo's figures than from medical books.

Vesalius' book, *On The Fabric of the Human Body*, was published in 1543. This was the same year Nicolas Copernicus, the Polish astronomer, published his book correctly describing how the sun, not the earth, is the center of the solar system. It is remarkable that two such breakthroughs in science should be made in the same year. Experts often date the start of the scientific revolution from this year, 1543.

The magnificent *Fabric* contained 663 pages and 300 beautiful illustrations. The drawings by Calcar were not only beautiful works of art, but correct as scientific drawings, too. They showed that the body is "fearfully and wonderfully made" as the Bible states in Psalm 139:14. Vesalius' book drew fierce opposition. Doctors who had taught Galen for so long felt their reputations were at stake. They pounced upon every small error in *Fabric* and hotly ridiculed Vesalius.

His old teacher, Sylvius, accused Vesalius of all sorts of crimes. He wrote a book against Vesalius. In it he said, "Let no one pay attention to that very ignorant man. He denies everything his deranged or feeble vision cannot locate." Scornfully, Sylvius titled his own book *Slanders of a Madman Against Galen*.

He even attacked Vesalius' use of illustrations. He felt the pictures made the textbook unprofessional and even childish. After all, Galen and the other ancient physicians did not illustrate their books. Galen taught solely by words.

Vesalius was just 28 when he published *Fabric*. He spent his personal fortune and all his enthusiasm on it. Eventually, his fame would be assured. It didn't happen soon enough for Vesalius personally.

Being a proud and ambitious man, Vesalius became infuriated that some professors didn't instantly recognize the importance of his book. Then, when the book did gain world recognition, he became infuriated all over again when publishers pirated his book. They published parts of it without his permission and pocketed the profit.

For the next 20 years Vesalius wasted his life in quarrels defending his work. He

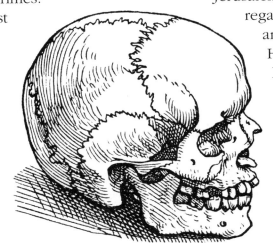

This drawing from Vesalius' book was considered to be the normal skull type. His drawings allowed other doctors to study anatomy without the need for dissection.

gave up his teaching position. His medical discoveries came to a halt. He wandered over Europe. At age 50 he traveled to Jerusalem. Perhaps he hoped to regain his former drive and ambition by visiting the Holy Land. A friend met him on the road to Jericho. After that, nothing else is known for certain about Vesalius' last days. We have no official record of where he died, when he died, or where he is buried.

What is left is the book *On the Fabric of the Body*. The publication of *Fabric* marked a turning point in the history of medicine. It is generally regarded as one of the ten most important events in medical science.

DIAGNOSES

1. Vesalius did not accept the teachings of Galen without experimenting on his own.

2. Vesalius learned human anatomy by looking at humans not just animals.

3. He made detailed drawings of his findings so others could also learn.

Answer T or F for true or false, or
select A or B for the phrase that best completes the sentence.

A B   1. Andreas Vesalius came from a long line of (A. doctors; B. lawyers).

T F   2. Vesalius' father discouraged Vesalius from doing medical experiments.

A B   3. Vesalius studied skeletons of humans while Galen had studied skeletons of (A. criminals, B. apes).

T F   4. At Padua, students paid the teachers' salaries.

T F   5. Vesalius' lectures were popular with the other medical professors at Padua.

T F   6. Vesalius' lectures were popular with the students at Padua.

A B   7. Those professors who opposed Vesalius believed (A. dissections served no purpose; B. Galen needed to be replaced).

T F   8. Vesalius' book was published the same year as Copernicus published his book putting the sun at the center of the solar system.

T F   9. Vesalius' use of illustrations drew swift praise from doctors who had taught Galen.

T F   10. When Vesalius died he was hailed as a hero and given a state funeral.

T F   11. Publication of *The Fabric of the Human Body* is considered one of the ten most important events in medical science.

Select the matching letter from the list below.

12. _____ was a young artist who made illustrations for Vesalius' book.

13. _____ was an artist who studied the human body so he could paint it accurately.

14. _____ was a Polish astronomer who described the sun and not the earth as the center of the planetary system.

15. _____ was a successful apothecary (druggist).

16. _____ taught in Paris from old books.

17. _____ wrote *On The Fabric of the Human Body*.

A. Andreas Vesalius
B. Jan Stephen van Calcar
C. Leonardo da Vinci
D. Nicolas Copernicus
E. Sylvius
F. Vesalius' father

Father of Modern Surgery

As Vesalius found out, professors in medical schools seldom performed surgery. They didn't think it proper for a professional man to do such work. The word surgeon is from a French word meaning "one who works with his hands."

This narrow-minded rejection of honest labor grew from the daily life of ancient Greece. The only people with leisure time — time to free their minds to think upon scientific problems — were members of the upper class.

Their slaves did all of the manual labor. Those of noble birth considered it disgraceful to dirty their hands in scientific experiments. They believed, incorrectly, that they could solve problems simply by thinking about them.

SYMPTOMS

1. Doctors used cruel and painful treatments.

2. Professional doctors thought that surgery was beneath them.

3. Medical textbooks were written in Latin so that the barber surgeons could not use them.

Can You Diagnose the Discoveries?

In Europe of the 1500s, barbers, not doctors, performed minor operations, pulled teeth, and treated cuts. Barbers who gained skill in closing wounds were called barber-surgeons. The stripes of a barber pole still show the red for blood and the white of bandages.

The greatest of the barber-surgeons was Ambroise Paré (pa-RAY).

Ambroise Paré was born in a country town in France in 1510. Born into a poor family, he received only a merchant's education. It did not include Latin and Greek, the languages used by scholars and doctors. His parents did teach Paré about the love of God. Throughout his life, he retained the simple humility that is so characteristic of all true Christians.

He grew up to be a barber's assistant. It was the first step to becoming a full-fledged doctor. As time passed Ambroise grew more and more interested in the medical side of his barber profession. In 1529, at the age of 19, he took a big step. He decided to become a real doctor.

"The best medical schools are in

The town barber who cut men's hair also attended to the town's basic medical needs. Ambroise Paré was trained as a barber-surgeon where he learned the practical aspects of medicine and surgery first hand. Even today, the red stripe of the barber pole (left) stands for blood and the white stripe for bandages.

Paris," Ambroise said to his parents. "I'll study there."

The medical schools in Paris turned him away. He couldn't pass their entrance examinations. He had the ability. Professors gave entrance tests in Latin and Greek, languages he could neither read nor write. At the time he was intensely disappointed. He said, "It did not please

God to favor my youth with instruction in one or the other languages."

He had come to Paris to study medicine. His strong spirit refused to be broken by the rejections. He found a position as barber-surgeon at the "Hotel of God." It was a charity hospital, the oldest hospital in the world and very primitive. The hospital building was dirty, poorly lighted, and damp. Charcoal fires burned in copper pans on the floor to heat it during winter.

Every so often, a professor would bring his medical students around to the wards and lecture to them about the cases there. The students wrinkled their noses at the foul smells of the sick. They fled from the place as soon as the lectures ended. It was much more pleasant to treat wealthy patients in their homes.

Ambroise Paré gained a tremendous amount of practical experience. He discovered that many of the facts the professors taught their students were wrong.

Ambroise Paré made many of his discoveries while operating on the battlefield. The soldiers were so impressed with his innovations to help relieve pain that they collected gold and silver in a helmet and gave it to him.

Everything Paré learned came to him firsthand.

Three years later, when France went to war, Paré was hired to be a surgeon.

Doctors of Paré's day taught that powder burns from gunshots were poisonous. "Such wounds will prove fatal unless treated at once," they declared. The treatment was a brutal one. They poured boiling oil into the wound to drive out the poison. This terrible remedy was horribly painful.

Paré followed the standard medical remedy until a fearful battle broke out. Many men fell from gunshot wounds. Paré ran out of oil. He had to treat the wounds somehow, so in desperation he made an ointment of egg yolk, oil of roses, and turpentine.

Then he dressed the wounds in the soothing ointment. Throughout the night he worried about the men. He blamed himself for running out of oil. He expected the patients not treated with boiling oil to die of the "powder burn poison." He hardly slept during the night.

The next morning he made the rounds. To his great relief he discovered that the men who had received soothing ointment had rested far more comfortably than those treated with boiling oil. They were alive, doing well, and feeling little pain.

"The others," he reported, "those treated with boiling oil, ran a high fever. Their wounds were inflamed, swollen, and acutely painful."

It wasn't acceptable medical practice, but, "Never again," Paré said. "I've resolved never so cruelly to burn poor wounded men."

This set him thinking about other ways to relieve pain. Hippocrates, the Greek physician, had taught that doctors should avoid harsh remedies. It was better to do nothing than to take drastic action. Many surgeons failed to remember that they were working on human beings. They cut away without regard for the pain they caused. Paré felt otherwise. "The foundation of medicine must be love," Paré said.

Paré's most horrible duty involved amputations of arms or legs. After an amputation, doctors seared the stump with a white hot iron. Otherwise the unfortunate victim would bleed to death. Often soldiers endured the amputation only to die from shock when Paré applied the hot iron.

Wasn't there a less painful way to stop the bleeding?

Paré thought of a simple, almost painless solution. He put a spool of silk thread in his medical kit.

The test came late one night when a stray bullet shattered a soldier's leg. Paré had no choice but to remove the leg — it was broken beyond repair. Unless he took immediate action, infection would set in, the limb would fester and end in certain death.

This was before painkillers. An amputation had to be done quickly. A surgeon's skill was judged by his speed. Paré made his incision and sawed through the bone in only three minutes. The soldier endured the amputation while fully awake, and bravely withstood Paré sawing through the bone. At the end of the operation, Paré's assistant handed him the hot iron.

"Not this time," Paré said and passed it back. Instead, he removed from his medical bag the silk thread. Working rapidly, Paré tied off the blood vessels. Bleeding stopped. As simple as that! The patient lived.

When other soldiers heard of the successful surgery, they made Paré

This ornate surgeon's knife from Parés book was used for amputating limbs. Without painkillers, speed was the most important skill of a surgeon.

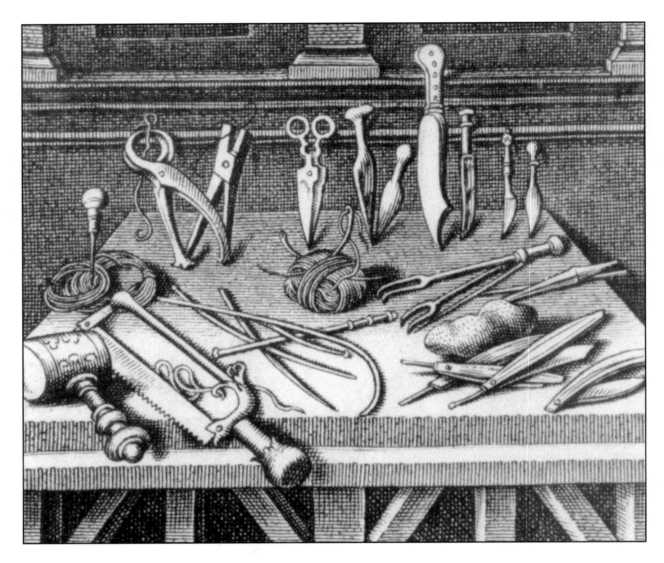

their hero. They loved the young surgeon who spared them from so much pain. Soldiers were very poorly paid, but they filled a helmet with silver and gold coins to reward him.

Ambroise Paré, as humble as ever, said, "I treated him. God healed him." Paré willingly tried new ways of healing. His methods saved thousands of soldiers who would have been left for dead on the battlefield. Paré refused to give up hope for an injured man. He said, "God often brings things to pass which seem impossible to the surgeon."

In Paris, however, doctors resented

These surgical instruments used by Paré were published in "The works of that famous surgeon Ambroise Parey Paré" in 1634. His surgical techniques were so popular with doctors and barber-surgeons alike that his books were published many times and in several different languages.

Ambroise Paré's success. A piece of thread did the work of a white hot iron! He closed cuts with needle and thread like a common housewife mending a tear in cloth.

One doctor warned, "To tie the vessels after amputation is a new remedy.

Therefore, it should not be used." Paré decided to write about his medical discoveries. Although he had learned Latin, he chose to write in French so common barber-surgeons could read his book.

The book was delightful. Rather than quoting ancient authorities, Paré packed his book with practical surgical advice. He never tried to use big words to sound more profound.

As important as Paré's manuscript was, he couldn't get it published. Doctors in the medical schools resented his fame. They were the experts, they believed, and Paré only a backward barber. An old law was found and used against Paré. No medical book could be published unless a committee of doctors from the medical schools of Paris approved it.

Four years passed before Paré got the necessary approval. Finally, his book was published. It sold out immediately. Barbers, and doctors, too, clamored for copies. The publisher reprinted it four times within a few years. It was translated into Latin and several other languages, including English.

Some people expressed surprise that he shared his medical knowledge so freely. His fame and livelihood came from the medical facts he put to work each day.

Paré answered: "The light of a candle will not diminish no matter how many may come to light their torches by it."

Paré met Vesalius in Paris and learned of his study of the human body. During a

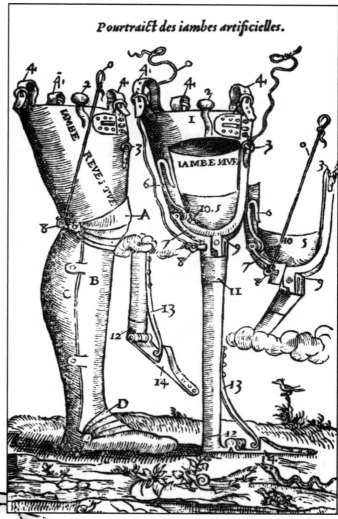

Pourtraiĉt des iambes artificielles.

One illustration from Paré's book (1575) shows an artificial leg with a movable joint at the knee and ankle (top).

Another from a later edition (1628) shows two artificial noses (left) made of leather with straps to tie them on.

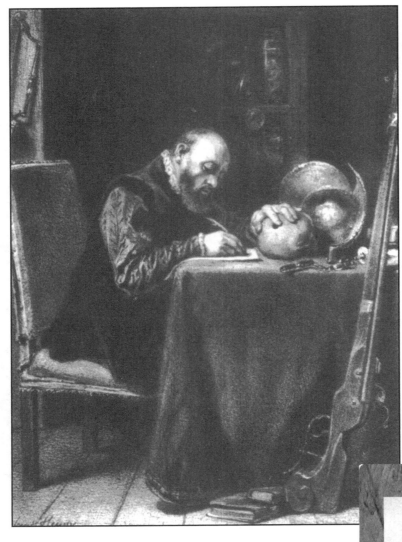

The barber-surgeon Ambroise Paré made a major impact on the world of medicine through his practical approach of helping people. He made more discoveries than many of the highly educated people of his day.

He never earned a medical degree. Yet he became France's most skilled surgeon. In 1562 he was given the dignified title, "First Surgeon of the King."

Paré died in 1590. He had practiced medicine to the last.

This humble barber-surgeon had replaced worthless speculation in surgery with practical experience. His discovery that blood vessels could be tied off to prevent bleeding marked the start of modern surgery.

Today the humble barber-surgeon is ranked as the founder of modern surgery. The people of France raised a statue in his honor. Inscribed on it are the simple words: "I treated him; God healed him."

tournament, a lance had hit the king in the head. The wound was so severe that neither Vesalius nor Paré could save him.

The king died. But Paré did learn of Vesalius's study of the human body.

Paré translated summaries of Vesalius' books into French. Other barber-surgeons would have a guide to the human body.

Paré did not have a formal education.

DIAGNOSES

1. Paré used ointments and silk thread to repair injuries in place of burning oil and hot pokers.

2. Paré discovered new techniques that made surgery practical.

3. He published his book in French with useful information that all doctors could use.

*Answer T or F for true or false, select A — D,
or fill in the blank for the phrase that best completes the sentence.*

A B C D   1. In Europe of the 1500s, minor operations and first aid were given by
(A. barbers; B. dentists; C. doctors; D. janitors).

T F   2. As a child Paré learned to read and write both Latin and Greek.

A B C   3. In Paris, Paré took a position at a
(A. teaching university; B. King's summer home; C. charity hospital).

A B C D   4. Paré's improved treatment for gunshot wounds was to
(A. pour in boiling oil; B. use soothing ointment; C. sear the wound
with a hot iron; D. use thread to tie the veins and arteries closed).

   5. Paré said, "The foundation of medicine must be _____."

A B C D   6. Paré's improved treatment to stop the bleeding after an amputation
was to (A. pour in boiling oil; B. use soothing ointment; C. sear the
wound with a hot iron; D. use thread to tie the veins and arteries closed).

   7. Ambroise Paré said, "I treated him, _____ healed him."

T F   8. Paré was reluctant to share his discoveries with others.

A B   9. Paré became France's most skilled surgeon and earned the title
(A. Master Barber; B. First Surgeon of the King).

The Living River

Ten years after the death of Paré, William Harvey of England traveled to Padua in Italy to study medicine. He was a short, intense young man. He had a round face, olive complexion, and bright eyes. His black hair always needed grooming.

Harvey found the university to be an exciting place. There he had time to study the writings of old physicians, and learn new discoveries. Galileo was the school's most famous teacher. Students packed the classroom to hear his dramatic lectures. Galileo's ideas took the scientific world by storm. Rather than depending upon the mere authority of ancient writers, Galileo insisted that experiments were the road to scientific truth. Galileo applied his new methods of scientific research to non-living things.

SYMPTOMS

1. Doctors were too dependent upon writings of old physicians.

2. Galen's writings were based upon false ideas about blood circulation.

Can You Diagnose the Discoveries?

William Harvey believed the same approach could be used to study medicine, too. The young Englishman became one of Padua's best-known students. The other students from England elected him president of the English student body.

William Harvey read the works of Hippocrates, Galen, and Vesalius. Although Vesalius proved Galen wrong about the construction of the human body, doctors of Padua still accepted his ideas on other matters. They still turned to Galen's books to look up the "right" answer.

Doctors believed veins carried blood away from the heart. The flow, according to the doctors and Galen, was slow and irregular. Blood ebbed and flowed like tides. Galen taught that the liver manufactured new blood to replace the old.

Unfortunately, Galen knew nothing about blood circulation. What he wrote he based upon completely false ideas. For example, he believed blood surging through the heart caused it to beat. He had no idea that the heart itself pumped blood.

William Harvey dared to question Galen's ideas on the circulation of blood. He studied Galileo's ideas that experiments were the road to scientific truth. Harvey believed the same approach could be used to study medicine.

David Fabricius (pronounced fa-BRISH-ee-use), successor to Vesalius, lectured on surgery and anatomy. He gave his demonstrations in a small amphitheater. Galleries rose in steep tiers nearly to the roof. Students stood at the railings. From there everyone had a good view of the little space in the center where Fabricius dissected the body. This design, of a steeply sloping row of seats around an operating table, is still used in medical teaching schools.

Fabricius pointed out valves, like little trap doors, in the veins.

The lectures impressed Harvey, especially those dealing with the heart, veins, and arteries. Harvey wondered about the purpose of the valves. Galen said blood in the veins always flowed away from the heart. Yet, these trap doors pointed the wrong way. According to the way they were constructed the blood would flow toward the heart. Something was wrong!

Fabricius had studied the valves. He couldn't explain them, either. "These little doors keep the blood from flowing out too rapidly," Fabricius explained lamely.

In 1602 William Harvey earned his medical degree and returned to England. He married and began a successful medical practice in London. He even became physician to King James I, who authorized a new translation of the Bible — the King James translation.

He continued to be fascinated by the problem of the heart and blood flow. After ten years of study, he'd not solved the mystery to his satisfaction. "I'm almost tempted to think," he said, "that the motion of the heart can only be comprehended by God."

Harvey didn't spin theories. He carried out simple but easily understood experiments.

In one experiment he tied off a vein. Blood caused the vein to bulge on one side, but the side nearest the heart drained empty. Veins carried blood to the heart! When he stopped the flow in an artery, the vessel always bulged on the side toward the heart. Arteries carried blood away from the heart.

He calculated that in one hour the heart pumps seven gallons of blood. The liver couldn't possibly make that much blood in an hour.

The ancient physician Galen was wrong again. Blood had to be reused, it couldn't just fade away. "Blood must move in a closed path. It circulates."

Each year the College of Physicians sponsored a series of lectures to keep London doctors in touch with new developments in their profession. In 1616 the College of Physicians invited William Harvey to speak. He lectured upon the circulation of blood. He said, "Thus is proved a perpetual motion of the blood

In this experiment of tying off veins in the arm, Harvey proved Galen was wrong about blood circulation. When he tied off a vein, the side nearest the heart drained empty. When he tied off an artery, the vessel always bulged on the side toward the heart. Through this simple experiment, Harvey proved that blood circulates through the body in one direction.

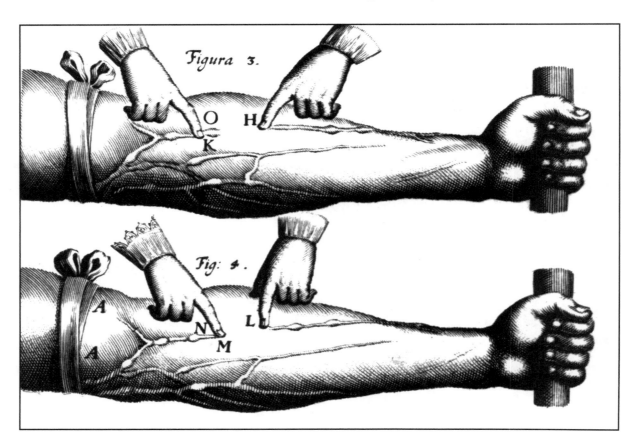

in a circle caused by the beating of the heart."

The lectures caused hardly a ripple in scientific circles. Doctors thought the short little man with the intense eyes was merely repeating what he'd learned in Italy. Besides, what did it matter? Would knowing about blood flow prevent disease?

We know now, of course, that blood

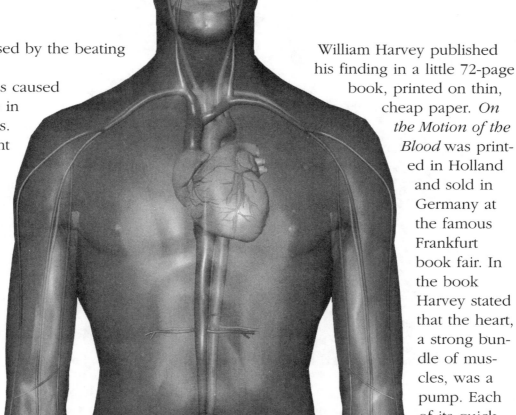

The heart is the muscle that pumps blood in a closed path through the body. The blood collects life-giving oxygen from the lungs and delivers it to the organs and to every cell of the body.

is the river of life. The average human body contains about six quarts of blood. During its circuit, blood passes through the lungs where it absorbs oxygen. It passes along the stomach and intestine where it absorbs food. The food and oxygen are taken throughout the body. Cells accept the nutrients and discharge wastes products into the blood. The blood circulates through the kidneys to be purified.

Doctors could not get very far in their war against physical disorders unless they understood circulation of the blood.

William Harvey put his knowledge to use to cure a patient suffering from a large tumor. He tied off the arteries supplying blood to the growth. It withered away.

William Harvey published his finding in a little 72-page book, printed on thin, cheap paper. *On the Motion of the Blood* was printed in Holland and sold in Germany at the famous Frankfurt book fair. In the book Harvey stated that the heart, a strong bundle of muscles, was a pump. Each of its quick, clutching motions drove blood outward through the arteries. When the heart relaxed, blood from the veins flowed back in to fill it again.

"How does blood flow from arteries to veins?" doctors asked.

Harvey admitted the truth. "I have never been able to trace any connection between the arteries and veins. Both arteries and veins divide and sub-divide into finer and finer vessels. The connections exist, but they are too small to see."

Like many great books, *On the Motion of the Blood* first suffered vicious attacks. Harvey met bitter ridicule. Doctors who envied him proved him wrong by quoting from Galen, but not by repeating his experiments. They called him "cracked brained" and frightened away his patients.

Harvey is explaining the circulation of the blood to Charles I. There are several members of the King's court, including a young boy, listening. Harvey proved that blood moved in a closed path. His discovery is considered one of the ten most important events in medicine.

were tiny blood vessels that connected the arteries to the veins. Malpighi named the tiny tubes capillaries.

The way Harvey arrived at his discovery is as important as the discovery itself. He didn't build air castles out of idle speculation. He based his answers upon hard scientific experimentation. He proved that blood moved in a closed path. He showed the exact path over which it moved. His discovery of the circulation of the blood is considered one of the ten most important events in medicine. In fact, many people consider it the greatest of all medical discoveries.

Harvey lived to be 80 years old, long enough to see his work taken seriously. During his old age the circulation of blood became accepted as the true picture. Even then no connections had been found between arteries and veins. Fellow doctors elected him president of the College of Physicians. He decided not to serve.

His book took its place along with *Fabric* by Vesalius as one of the greatest medical books ever written.

The final piece of the puzzle fell into place just four years after Harvey's death. In 1661, an Italian physician named Marcello Malpighi (pronounced mahl-PEE-gee) put the recently invented microscope into use. He examined a slice of lung from a frog. There, as Harvey predicted,

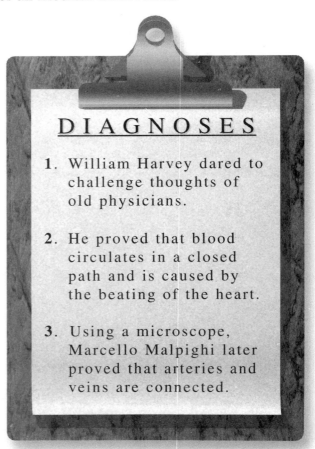

DIAGNOSES

1. William Harvey dared to challenge thoughts of old physicians.

2. He proved that blood circulates in a closed path and is caused by the beating of the heart.

3. Using a microscope, Marcello Malpighi later proved that arteries and veins are connected.

Questions

The Living River

Answer T or F for true or false, select A or B, or fill in the blank for the phrase that best completes the sentence.

A B 1. When William Harvey attended Padua in Italy, its most famous teacher was (A. Isaac Newton; B. Galileo).

T F 2. William Harvey believed that experiments could be used to study medicine.

A B 3. Blood is carried to the heart by (A. arteries; B. veins).

A B 4. When William Harvey tied closed an artery, it bulged on the side (A. toward; B. away) from the heart.

5. William Harvey stated that the heart was a ______________.

T F 6. Before he died, William Harvey's idea that blood circulates was accepted as the true picture.

T F 7. William Harvey discovered the connection between arteries and veins and named them capillaries.

T F 8. Today, Harvey's discovery of the circulation of blood is one of the ten most important events in medical discovery.

Write the letter of the matching choice.

9. _____ taught the experimental method at Padua.

10. _____ lectured on surgery and anatomy, pointed out valves in the veins.

11. _____ wrote *On the Motion of the Blood.*

12. _____ discovered capillaries.

A. David Fabricius
B. Galileo
C. Marcello Malpighi
D. William Harvey

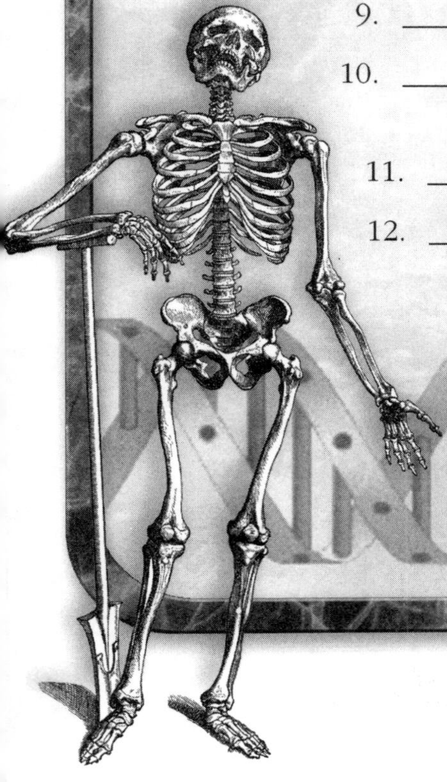

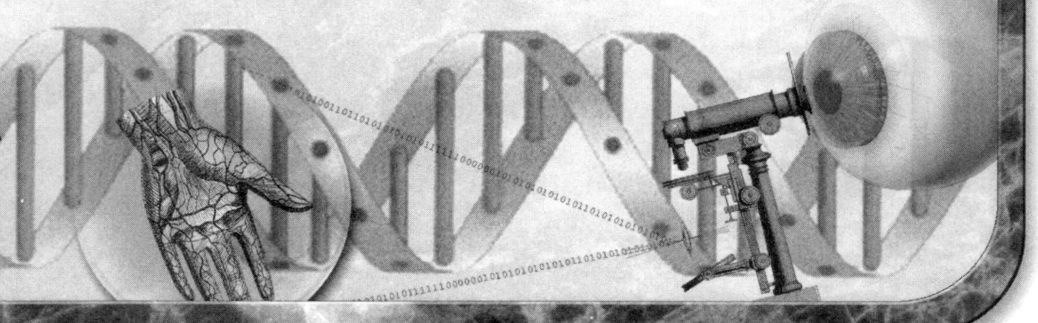

The Invisible Kingdom

Afer Gutenberg invented the printing press in 1450, books became much more common. For the first time, many people were able to read. To see a page of fine print, a person will bring the page closer to his eyes. The letters look bigger and can be read more easily. However, there is a limit. Once the page is brought too close, the person can no longer focus upon the print. The letters become blurred.

In addition, some people are far-sighted. They can see objects clearly at a distance, but cannot focus on fine print up close. People who cannot read small letters solve the problem by using a reading lens. This lens is thicker in the middle than at its edge. It does

SYMPTOMS

1. The Black Death plague was killing as many as one in three people.

2. Physicians could only study things that could be seen with the human eye.

3. Physicians did not know how to prevent the spread of deadly diseases.

Can You Diagnose the Discoveries?

not magnify much, only about two and a half times. Through a magnifying lens, a dime is about the size of a quarter.

The power of a magnifying lens increases as the lens is made smaller and more sharply curved. Such lenses require extreme care to grind and polish. Using them takes just as much care because the tiny lenses must be held nearly touching the eye.

A microscope made of a single small but powerful lens is known as a simple lens microscope. The word microscope is from micro, meaning "small," and scope, meaning "to see."

The greatest maker and user of simple lens microscopes was Antoni van Leeuwenhoek. He was not a professional scientist at all. He was completely self-taught. Perhaps it was just as well. Science during his time was pretty much filled with nonsense.

Antoni van Leeuwenhoek (pronounced LAY-ven-hook) was born in 1632 in Delft, Holland. While still a boy, Antoni's father died. Antoni left school at 16 to be an apprentice in a dry-goods store in Amsterdam. At age 21 he

Antoni van Leeuwenhoek was born in 1632 in Delft, Holland. He made microscopes and examined everything he could. Although some scoffed at his hobby, it would lead to one of the greatest medical discoveries of all time.

returned to Delft to open a dry-goods store of his own. Later, he was appointed janitor of the city hall.

His business brought him a comfortable income. In his spare time, he made microscopes — the best in the world. He kept after his hobby with a single-minded determination for more than 50 years.

He examined everything that he came across: cloth, hair, skin, fish scales, the wings of butterflies, and pieces of cork. He left his favorite subjects mounted in front of his lens. When he wanted to look at another object he ground another lens. He made about 550 microscopes in all. Leeuwenhoek wrote about his discoveries,

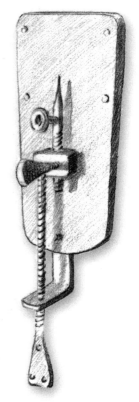

Antoni van Leeuwenhoek's first microscope with which he explored the unseen world.

not in learned Latin, but in everyday Dutch. It was the only language he knew. The letters were chatty with personal details. In 1674 he sent a letter to the Royal Society of England.

The learned men of the Royal Society couldn't make head nor tail of his work at first. Once they read past the chatty asides, it became clear the man knew what he was talking about. The Royal Society urged Leeuwenhoek to keep them informed of his activities.

In 1677, Leeuwenhoek saw tiny moving things in water from a nearby canal. They could not be seen with the eyes alone. He sat back astonished. This couldn't be! All scientists of his time knew that the tiny insect called a cheese-mite was the smallest of all creatures.

Leeuwenhoek found a fantastic world of little creatures in a drop of water. He wrote to the Royal Society: "I must say for my part, that no more pleasant sight has

Leeuwenhoek used a later model microscope (left) to study microscopic life and then sketched what he saw so that other people would believe him. These drawings were of creatures which no person had seen before (bottom left and next page).

ever yet come before my eyes. I judge that some of these little creatures are a thousand times smaller than the smallest mite."

At first, members of the Royal Society did not believe his reports. Christiaan Huygens, a famous maker of lenses, was one of those who objected. But he was willing to repeat Leeuwenhoek's experiments. "I was wrong," Christiaan Huygens admitted. "The little animals do exist."

Leeuwenhoek looked for the little animals everywhere. He peered at canal water, stew broth, even scrapings from his cheek inside his mouth. Everywhere he found little animals — even in drinking water!

What he had seen were one-celled animals now called protozoa. By simple arithmetic he calculated that a single drop of water would be home to one million of the little animals!

The English writer Jonathan Swift summed up Leeuwenhoek's discoveries in a famous poem:

So, naturalists observe, a flea
Hath smaller fleas that on them prey;
And these have smaller still to bite'em
And so proceed ad infinitum.

The phrase "ad infinitum" means "to infinity" or "so on forever."

More than once Leeuwenhoek expressed his humble admiration of the Creator who could fill a drop of water with such intricate life. He always referred to God as the Maker of the Great All.

In 1683, Leeuwenhoek made extremely powerful lenses no bigger than a pinhead. These lenses gave magnification of two hundred times. At the very limit of their power, he saw little rod-shaped bodies that moved and grew. They were even smaller than the little animals.

Leeuwenhoek's discoveries made him famous. The Royal Society and French Academy of Science elected him a member.

The Queen of England paid a visit to peer through his microscope. So did Peter the Great, ruler of all Russia.

Some of the local people, however, looked upon the strange man and complained. They thought he wasted his time. "We suffer from disease," they cried, "while he plays with a useless hobby!"

Leeuwenhoek's work eventually led to the discovery of the causes of diseases such as the Black Death. The Black Death, or bubonic plague, would sweep across the country, killing as many as one in three persons. For example, in 1665 the Black Death struck London. Ten thousand people died in a single month. Doctors were helpless. Frightened people fled

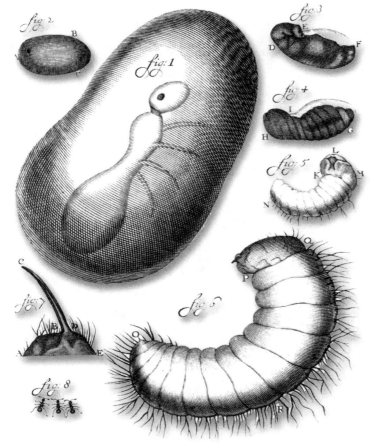

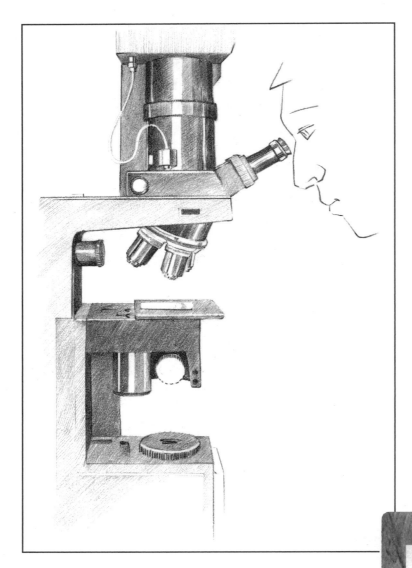

from rats onto humans and spread the disease.

Two hundred years would pass before doctors realized the role of bacteria in making people sick. But once this fact became known, the microscope became a permanent tool of medical research. Leeuwenhoek pursued his hobby for 50 years, until his death at age 90. He kept the Royal Society informed. He wrote hundreds of letters to them.

What made Leeuwenhoek so special? He exercised a single-minded determination to present exactly what he observed. More than a hundred years passed before other scientists glimpsed some of the things he saw, described, and sketched.

A modern electron microscope enables scientists to see viruses, the smallest form of life. Electron Microscopes are thousands of times more powerful than Leeuwenhoek's most advanced microscope.

from the overcrowded cities into the countryside. One town leader said, "Shut your doors against your friends, and if a man passeth over the fields avoid him as you would in time of war."

The small living things that Leeuwenhoek barely glimpsed are bacteria. No one knew or suspected it, but these tiny germs caused many diseases. A certain type of bacteria carried by rats caused the Black Death. Fleas jumped

DIAGNOSES

1. Leeuwenhoek developed the most powerful microscopes of his day.

2. He discovered one-celled protozoans and bacteria.

3. His work eventually led to the discovery of the causes of diseases, such as the Black Death.

Questions
The Invisible kingdom

Answer T or F for true or false, or
Select A – D for the phrase that best completes the sentence.

A B C D 1. The word micro means (A. to cook; B. to see; C. small; B. magnify).

T F 2. Leeuwenhoek worked as a janitor of the city hall.

A B 3. Leeuwenhoek wrote about his discoveries in (A. Dutch; B. Latin).

T F 4. The Royal Society refused to read Leeuwenhoek's letters.

A B 5. Leeuwenhoek made 550 microscopes because (A. he kept trying to get one he liked; B. he kept his favorite subjects mounted in front of his lens).

A B 6. The Black Death was caused by (A. a certain type of bacteria; B. lack of exercise; C. lack of sunlight; D. poor nutrition).

Write the letter of the matching choice.

7. _____ invented the printing press.
8. _____ said, "I was wrong. The little animals do exist."
9. _____ wrote a poem about Leeuwenhoek's discoveries.
10. _____ said, "We suffer from disease while he plays with a useless hobby!"
11. _____ said, "Shut your doors against your friends."
12. _____ referred to God as the Maker of the Great All.

A. Christiaan Huygens
B. Gutenberg
C. Jonathan Swift
D. Leeuwenhoek
E. The local people
F. The town leader when the Black Death struck

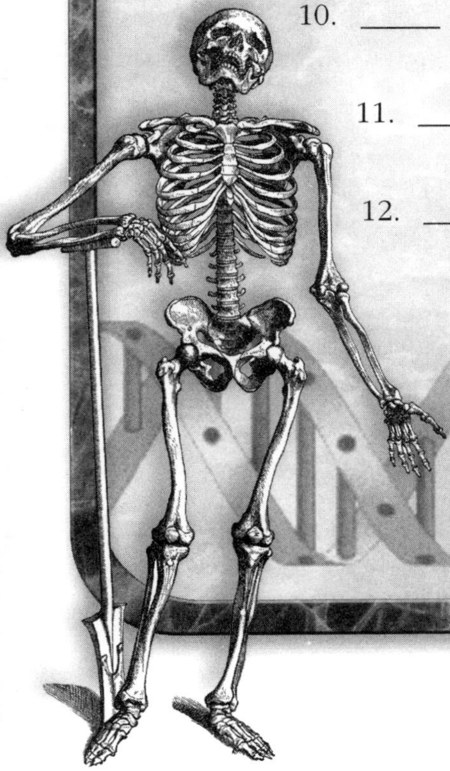

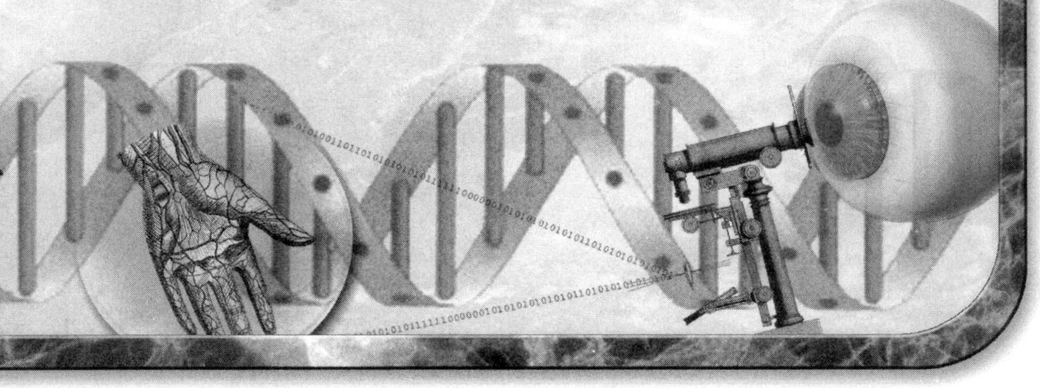

Triumph Over Smallpox

For centuries doctors merely treated diseases. They did little to prevent them. For example, from the earliest times until the late 1700s, smallpox was a common disease and a frightening one. It terrorized the whole world. Doctors regarded it as the most dreadful disease to strike human beings, worse than cholera, Black Death, or yellow fever. When it struck at full strength, as many as one out of three victims died.

Those who escaped death faced other consequences. Smallpox left some victims blind or deaf. It also caused miserable sores that left awful pockmarks. The worst cases disfigured faces beyond recognition. Some people could not bear to look at themselves in the mirror.

SYMPTOMS

1. For centuries doctors only treated diseases and did little to prevent them.

2. Thousands were dying from smallpox.

3. If a person survived smallpox, they might be left disfigured, blind or deaf.

Can You Diagnose the Discoveries?

Those who did survive smallpox could count themselves fortunate in one way. They could never fall victim to the disease again. For that reason, a very mild case of smallpox was far better than none at all. Many people preferred to have the disease and survive than to be forever afraid it might strike them next.

Some parents intentionally exposed their children to mild cases of smallpox. They hoped their children would come down with a mild case, too. It was risky business. Children in good health usually lived. Children in poor health often died.

Edward Jenner grew up in the village of Berkeley, England. He was the son of a clergyman, but lost his father and mother at age five. An older brother raised him and sent him to medical school in London.

When Edward Jenner finished his formal studies, he proved to be a well-trained doctor and very intelligent scientist. England's greatest scientific body, the Royal Society, elected him a member. Captain James Cook, the famous explorer of the South Seas, invited him to come along as the ship's natural scientist. Edward Jenner turned down Captain Cook's offer. Instead, he chose to live in Berkeley, the quiet village he loved.

A country girl who worked on a farm as a milkmaid told Edward she didn't need to worry about smallpox. "I've had cowpox," she explained. "It's a harmless disease and protects me from smallpox."

Cowpox was a mild disease common to cattle. Milkmaids who milked the cows often came down with it. It resembled smallpox in some ways. Country people around Berkeley believed that those who caught cowpox were forever free of not only cowpox but of smallpox, too.

Another person might have brushed aside the girl's story. Edward Jenner took the tale to Dr. Daniel Ludlow who had

Edward Jenner, the son of a clergyman, grew up in the village of Berkeley, England. After watching many of those around him die from smallpox, he was determined to find a way to fight this deadly disease.

SMALLPOX
KEEP OUT OF THIS HOUSE

By Order of BOARD OF HEALTH

HEALTH OFFICER

Any person removing this card without authority is liable to prosecution.

739 Market Street

instructed Edward in medicine. Dr. Ludlow was amused that the girl believed an animal disease could protect her from a human disease. "It's a silly superstition," the doctor said. "There is no truth in the girl's story."

Edward Jenner couldn't put the idea out of his mind. As the years passed, he checked out every reported case of smallpox or cowpox around the village. He did find milkmaids who could care for smallpox victims without fear for their own safety. They never caught smallpox. These lowly milkmaids enjoyed beautiful complexions, while highborn ladies suffered disfigurement from smallpox.

Yet, some people who had cowpox later caught smallpox. Were the milkmaids mistaken? Could the whole thing be nothing more than an old wives' tale without any basis in fact?

Many years passed before Edward Jenner understood completely. He uncovered the secret when he discovered more than one type of cowpox. Only a specific type of cowpox at a certain time during its development protected from smallpox.

About this time Mrs. John Phipps, one of the local women, came to Dr. Jenner.

A Board of Health quarantine poster warns that the premises are contaminated by smallpox. Isolation was a common practice to try to prevent the spread of the smallpox disease.

She pleaded with him to protect her young son. Little Jamie was often sick. He had been so sickly as an infant that she hadn't followed the usual practice of letting him contract a mild case of smallpox. "Now I'm afraid Jamie will be too weak to survive the next outbreak of smallpox."

A few days later a milkmaid named Sarah Nelmes came to Edward Jenner with a bad case of cowpox. The farmer she worked for sent her to Dr. Jenner for treatment. He had been waiting for such an opportunity. On May 14, 1796, he opened one of the cowpox blisters on Sarah's hand. He made two small cuts on Jamie Phipps' arm. He inserted fluid from the cowpox blister into the scratches.

After several days the boy came down with harmless cowpox, as Edward knew he would. The boy grew restless. He complained of a headache, and his arm got sore. But the scratches healed, leaving a small scar. Jamie became strong again.

Two months later Edward Jenner took the fateful step. He intentionally gave the boy smallpox. He scratched the boy's skin and rubbed fluid from a smallpox blister into it. If he failed, and the boy died of smallpox, people would call him a murderer. He would deserve that name. Twenty years of study and tests had convinced him what the outcome would be.

When people in the village found out about the experiment, they called Edward Jenner a cow doctor. One night someone threw rocks through his windows.

Little Jamie didn't die. He didn't even become sick. The people of Berkeley saw Jamie running about and playing like a normal child. The townspeople who knew Dr. Jenner rallied to his defense. They trusted him.

Within a few months other people knocked on Dr. Jenner's door. They asked for their children to be protected from smallpox. He hollowed out goose quills to carry cowpox serum around with him. He inoculated many of the local people.

Edward Jenner did the first inoculation on a healthy boy. He took serum from a cowpox sore on a milkmaid's hand and injected it into the boy. Jenner believed the harmless cowpox virus would make the boy's body build a resistance to the deadly smallpox virus. When Jenner later injected the boy with smallpox virus, the boy survived the killer disease.

Edward Jenner coined the word vaccination to describe his course of action. Vacca is the Latin word for cow.

That same year, in 1796, he packed his notes and several goose quills of serum. He took the samples to the London Smallpox Hospital. The head doctor turned him away. "I'm the world's authority on smallpox," the doctor said. "I know there is no way to prevent the disease."

Edward Jenner visited other hospitals. Everywhere he heard the same thing. "Nonsense," the doctors said. "You'll cause children to look like cows." Edward wrote a paper about his discovery. He sent it to the Royal Society for publication. They returned his paper with a stern letter. "We are doing you a favor by not publishing it," they explained. "It might ruin your reputation."

After two frustrating years, Edward Jenner decided to publish a book himself telling of his wonderful discovery. He paid to have the 75-page book published.

Normally, such a self-published book would have been ignored. But it made an immediate sensation. People who feared smallpox were desperate enough to try anything. Within 18 months, twelve thousand people in London alone were vaccinated.

Dr. Jenner wanted to return to his country practice, but the British Parliament voted him a reward of 10,000 pounds. At that time a working person earned about 100 pounds a year. They asked him to stay in London and train other doctors. The British royal family was vaccinated. Napoleon, the French general, ordered all soldiers in his armies to be vaccinated. In America, Thomas Jefferson, president of the United States, was vaccinated, as were members of his family.

Edward Jenner was ridiculed and resented by his fellow doctors. This cartoon makes fun of Jenner's inoculations. In a crowded room a physician (Jenner) prepares to vaccinate a young woman sitting in a chair. The scene about them is mayhem as several former patients demonstrate the effects of the vaccine with cows sprouting from various parts of their bodies.

However, English doctors didn't hasten to honor Edward Jenner. At first they laughed at him. One cartoon showed vaccinated people sprouting cow horns and talking in moos. These powerful physicians resented the country doctor who had turned the world upside-down with his discoveries.

Edward Jenner was nominated to the College of Physicians. The doctors agreed to admit him only after he took a test over the teachings of Hippocrates and Galen. Edward decided it was time to oppose the study of old, out-of-date doctors. He refused to take the test. In turn, the College of Physicians refused to elect him to the College.

Edward Jenner didn't mind. Vaccination caused smallpox to become a rare disease. Before his success, doctors spent exhausting and sleepless nights with patients dying of smallpox. Today, most doctors have never even seen a case of the disease. Except for a few carefully guarded samples in research laboratories, the germs that cause smallpox have been completely wiped off the face of the earth.

The country doctor found himself the most talked-about person in the world. After a year he was happy to go home again and return to the life of a country doctor. The years passed quickly in rural Berkeley. Each year brought new honors to his name. In parts of the world May 14, the day Edward Jenner performed the first vaccination, became a national holiday.

The Indians of North America had been free of the disease until it was brought over to the New World by European settlers. Then it struck them especially hard, wiping out entire settlements. Dr. Jenner's vaccination protected Native Americans from the disease once again.

The chiefs of Five Indian Nations in Canada wrote Edward Jenner, "We shall not fail to teach our children to speak the

Mothers brought their children (mostly infants) for inoculations from smallpox. Jenner's discovery saved many lives in many lands. In parts of the world May 14, the day Edward Jenner did the first vaccination, became a national holiday.

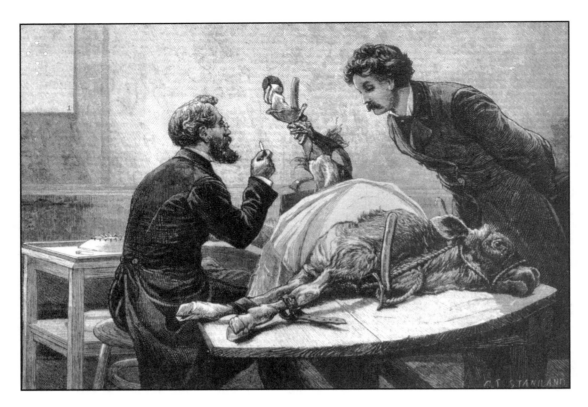

Doctors didn't suspect that weakened germs could actually help the body. Seventy-five years would pass before they conquered another disease. Edward Jenner's discovery of vaccination is considered one of the top ten medical discoveries of all time.

A physician is removing lymph from a calf. The lymph was then used to make the vaccine to prevent a person from having the disease of smallpox.

name of Jenner; and to thank the Great Spirit for bestowing upon him so much wisdom and so much love. We beseech the Great Spirit to take care of you in this world and in the land of the Spirits."

Edward Jenner died in 1823. One bitterly cold day in January he walked to a nearby village to arrange for fuel to be given to the poor. Upon his return home he went to bed. He died the next day, probably because of exposure to bad weather.

People in all lands accepted Dr. Jenner's inoculation, or "shots," against smallpox. Neither he nor any other doctor knew the cause of infectious diseases or why vaccination worked. We know now that vaccination is done with weakened germs. The person treated gets a mild and harmless form of the disease. The body sets up an immunity to it.

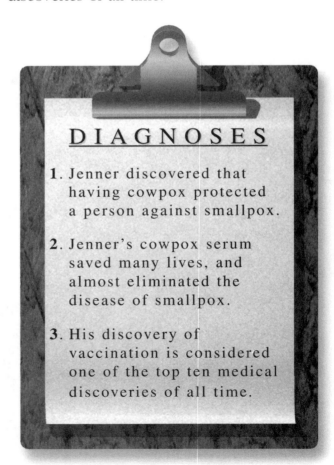

DIAGNOSES

1. Jenner discovered that having cowpox protected a person against smallpox.

2. Jenner's cowpox serum saved many lives, and almost eliminated the disease of smallpox.

3. His discovery of vaccination is considered one of the top ten medical discoveries of all time.

Answer T or F for true or false, or
Select A — D for the phrase that best completes the sentence.

T F 1. Those who survived smallpox had beautiful, clear skin.

T F 2. A person could get smallpox time and again.

A B C D 3. The milkmaid believed that those who had cowpox
(A. became blind and deaf; B. never fell victim to smallpox;
C. suffered from constant headaches; D. were left with horrible pockmarks).

T F 4. After giving the boy cowpox, Jenner waited two months and gave him smallpox.

A B C D 5. Vacca is a word meaning (A. a needle; B. cow; C. inoculation; D. small).

T F 6. The Royal Society was the first to publish Edward Jenner's paper about his discovery.

T F 7. The British royal family was vaccinated.

T F 8. The College of Physicians was the first medical group to honor Jenner.

Write the letter of the matching choice.

1. _____ invited Jenner along as ship's natural scientist.
2. _____ said, "It [cowpox] is a harmless disease and protects me from smallpox."
3. _____ said, "It's a silly superstition."
4. _____ was the first person to be vaccinated against smallpox.
5. _____ said, "I know there is no way to prevent the disease [smallpox]."
6. _____ ordered his soldiers to be vaccinated.
7. _____ said, "We beseech the Great Spirit to take care of you."

A. The chiefs of the Five Indian Nations in Canada
B. Dr. Daniel Ludlow
C. The head doctor at London Smallpox Hospital
D. James Cook
E. James Phipps
F. The milkmaid
G. Napoleon

Davy Deadens Pain

In the early 1800s, surgery seemed more like torture than a medical procedure. Pain made anything but the simplest surgery a terrible agony.

Some doctors gave their patients drugs like opium and morphine. To deaden pain this way during surgery turned out in the long run to be as bad as the pain itself. Many a surgeon caused his patients to become drug addicts. Drugs were simply too dangerous.

Other doctors filled the patient with whiskey in the hope the patient would pass out. Whiskey did not provide any true insensitivity to pain. Patients sobered in a hurry once the blade sliced through their flesh. Alcohol simply didn't work.

By the start of the 1800s all of these methods had fallen into disfavor. Instead, doctors

SYMPTOMS

1. Pain of surgery was almost unbearable.

2. Pain-relieving drugs caused addiction.

3. Pain of surgery required speed over accuracy.

Can You Diagnose the Discoveries?

performed surgery with the patient fully awake. The skill of a surgeon was measured by how quickly he worked, not by how well he did the job. Operations seldom lasted more than five minutes. Most were over in less than a minute. A British surgeon routinely took off a leg in a minute or less.

One man described such an operation: "With one sweep of his knife the surgeon cut off the limb of his patient, three fingers of his assistant, and the coattail of a spectator." The man who told this story was only joking. His story did point out how fast surgeons worked.

The pain affected kindhearted doctors almost as much as it did their patients. They couldn't face the agony inflicted upon their patients. Many doctors gave up surgery to follow another career.

Although pain is unpleasant, it usually serves a purpose. It calls attention to trouble inside your body. Without pain you would be unable to feel heat, cold, and pressure. You could bang your leg, cut it, and bleed to death without feeling anything.

As a teenager, Humphry Davy worked in one of the first pneumatic hospitals. His experience with using gases for medicine would lead him to search for a better painkiller.

For instance, one of the problems lepers face is the loss of sensation. The disease attacks their nerves. Lepers can't feel pain or heat in their hands or fingers. If a leper were to hold a tin cup filled with scalding hot water, he could suffer bad burns and not even be aware of it.

Pain during surgery is certainly unwelcome. Some operations can't be rushed. Until the discovery of painkillers, known as anesthetics, in the 1850s, doctors did operations at breakneck speed.

The story of painkillers actually begins with the discovery of gases. Earth's atmosphere is made of a mixture of gases, mostly oxygen and nitrogen. In the 1700s, chemists discovered other gases like hydrogen and carbon dioxide.

Some doctors believed gases helped their patients. They opened pneumatic hospitals. Pneumatic is a word meaning "air." Patients came to breathe these new gases. Inhaling various gases was supposed to cure all sorts of diseases. Of course, this treatment was worthless.

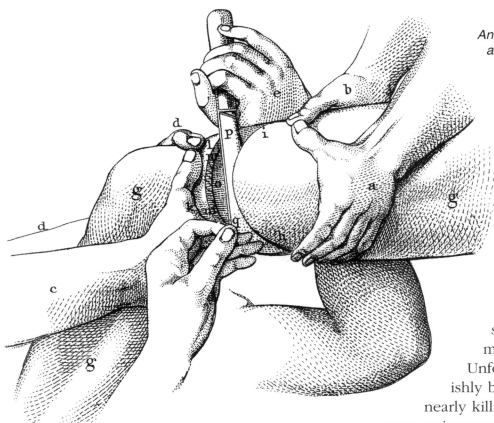

An illustration of a leg being amputated without any anesthesia. The skill of a surgeon was measured by how quickly he worked, not by how well he did the job. A British surgeon routinely took off a leg in a minute or less.

A teenager named Humphry Davy worked in one of the first pneumatic hospitals. Humphry Davy came from a wealthy family, or so he thought. Upon the death of his father, the family fortune turned out to be a large family debt. Humphry Davy was a Christian. He felt it his duty to make good on the debt. He became an apprentice to an apothecary (druggist) and, bit by bit, repaid everyone.

Humphry Davy turned to chemistry full time in 1797. Dr. Thomas Beddoes hired him to investigate the medical properties of various gases. Davy showed considerable talent in making new gases. Unfortunately, he foolishly breathed each one, nearly killing himself with the more poisonous ones.

Humphry Davy's first medical triumph was his discovery of laughing gas. The gas, nitrous oxide, is the chemical combination of two

Humphry Davy's gas machine allowed the patient to breath laughing gas or nitrous oxide. In addition to producing strong fits of laughter, it could also be used to relieve pain.

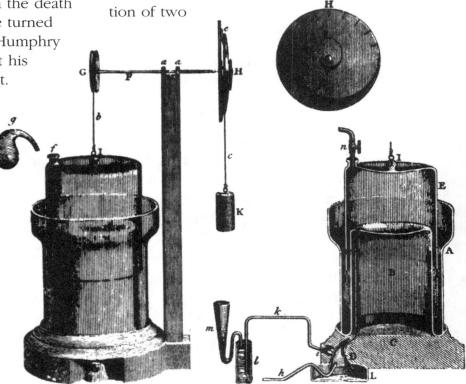

nitrogen atoms and one oxygen atom. Davy reported that the gas, when breathed, caused him to feel light-headed. He couldn't control his emotions. He would have a crying binge or laughing jig.

One day his employer called Davy from the laboratory to make the medical rounds. Unknown to Dr. Beddoes, Davy had been testing nitrous oxide. As the patients described their ailments, Davy responded with howls of laughter. Finally, Davy was led from the hospital, giggling out of control.

Davy was the first scientist to give public lectures about his discoveries. Ordinary people could learn about science. His lectures included dramatic displays of electricity, exploding gases, and so on. Eventually he became England's best-known scientist.

Unfortunately, Davy's habit of sniffing and tasting new chemicals left him physically disabled. Then, in 1812, an explosion nearly blinded him. There was nothing wrong with his mind. He hired an assistant named Michael Faraday. Together, they continued to make first-rate discoveries.

"It appears to me that laughing gas is capable of destroying physical pain," Davy stated. "It overcame a toothache that I had. Maybe it can be used during surgical operations." Humphry Davy was a chemist, not a doctor, so he did nothing else with the new gas.

We know now that nitrous oxide alone is not powerful enough to be used for general surgery. Most patients still feel some pain. For that reason, Davy's discovery finds its greatest use by dentists who must pull teeth. It is also used in combination with other painkillers.

The next step toward painless surgery in England was taken by James Young Simpson. As the seventh son of a poor baker, his future looked bleak. The family decided upon an unusual experiment. They picked the boy with the most promise — James — and put the family savings at his disposal. As he grew older, he could support the others in the family.

Sir James Young Simpson was not only a doctor, but also a Christian and a Bible scholar. He answered the medical objections to anesthesia and justified its use based on Genesis 2:21.

Young James didn't disappoint them. He started school at age 4, entered medical college at age 14, and became a doctor at age 21.

Most doctors practiced their profession by repeating unproven remedies. Not Simpson. He studied all areas of medicine. He tested what he studied. Because of his success, he became a professor of medicine at the University of Edinburgh. He peppered his lectures with the latest scientific facts. For example, he encouraged students to use microscopes to examine diseased tissue. This put him at odds with older doctors. Once, Simpson's boss shook his fist at Simpson and shouted, "I don't believe one word of your lecture!"

In 1846, James Simpson read reports of ether being used in America as an anesthetic. He tried it on his patients.

Simpson and his colleagues are experimenting on themselves with chloroform. Unfortunately, this practice could be very dangerous. Davy's experiments on himself left him physically disabled, and an explosion nearly blinded him.

Simpson had only limited success. He used sulfuric ether and not the purer form of diethyl ether. Because of impurities, sulfuric ether couldn't be depended on to give uniform results. It didn't work the same from one patient to the next or even on the same patient from one day to the next. Also, ether carried a suffocating odor that repelled patients. They struggled against the doctor as he tried to administer the gas. Ether had the habit of exploding at the slightest spark. Doctors handled it with care or blew up the operating room.

Because of these dangers, Simpson searched for a replacement. After dozens of trials, he hit upon chloroform. Chloroform is a sweet-smelling, colorless liquid that readily evaporates. It is the chemical combination of one carbon atom, one hydrogen atom and three chlorine atoms. Carbon is the main element that makes up coal. Chlorine is one of the elements found in ordinary table salt.

Simpson urged other doctors to use chloroform. He held up his hand and ticked off its advantages. "One, chloroform does not explode or even burn. Two, it works in a predictable way. Three, and best of all, it possesses a rather sweet smell. I can give it to my patients by simply pouring some on a handkerchief and holding it under their noses."

Simpson summed up its advantages, "Chloroform works faster than ether and is easier for the patient to take."

Some doctors refused to use chloroform or any other anesthetic. They said,

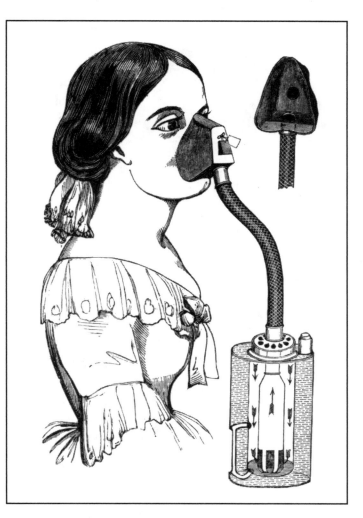

A patient is using a chloroform inhaler. Simpson fought hard to convince other doctors that chloroform was the best anesthetic. He argued that chloroform worked faster than ether and was easier for the patient to take because of its sweet smell.

"Pain serves a purpose. It is wrong to try to avoid pain." Some clergymen agreed with this view. Those who opposed painkillers fought a hard battle against James Simpson.

If anyone could answer these objections, it was James Simpson. He was not only a doctor, but a Christian and Bible scholar, too. He wrote religious pamphlets calling people to follow Christ. In one pamphlet he told of the greatest discovery he ever made: the discovery of Jesus Christ as his Savior. "I must tell others about Him," Simpson wrote. " 'With His stripes we are healed.' "

He not only answered the medical objections to anesthesia, but justified its use on biblical grounds, too. "God does not rejoice in pain," Simpson pointed out. "Recall how he removed the rib from Adam to make Eve." He quoted the Bible verse from Genesis 2:21 that says, "And the Lord God

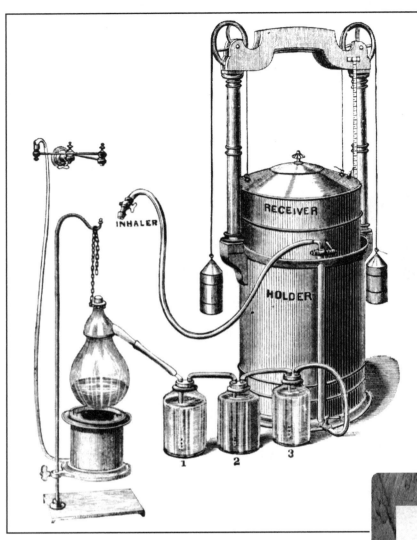

An apparatus from the 19th century to purify gas in the preparation of laughing gas (nitrous oxide). This involves a series of bottles for agitating and washing the gas. These bottles are connected to a tank by tube, as is a nozzle for inhalation of the purified gas.

was his fight to make anesthesia an established part of surgery.

The use of chloroform, however, turned out to be a dead end. Although chloroform does not burn or explode, the chemical is a poison and may cause cancer. A few patients suffer heart attacks when they breathe it.

Nitrous oxide and chloroform proved to be false starts on the road to modern painkillers. Success would come in a country that European doctors looked upon as backward and hardly civilized — the upstart United States.

caused a deep sleep to fall upon Adam and he slept; and he took one of his ribs, and closed up the flesh instead thereof."

Simpson said, "Here is the first surgical operation. God himself chose to perform it with the patient under anesthesia."

Queen Victoria showed her support by appointing him her personal physician. Dr. Simpson's greatest gift to medicine

DIAGNOSES

1. Humphry Davy discovered laughing gas which has made dentistry much less painful.

2. James Young Simpson discovered chloroform could be used as an anesthetic.

3. Simpson fought to make anesthesia an established part of surgery.

Answer T or F for true or false, or
Select A — D for the phrase that best completes the sentence.

T F   1. Surgeons who gave their patients opium and morphine ran the risk of causing their patients to become drug addicts.

T F   2. Whiskey proved to be an effective painkiller.

A B C D   3. By the start of the 1800s, the skill of a surgeon was judged by (A. his income; B. how fast he worked; C. where he attended medical school; D. whether he used opium or whiskey to deaden pain).

A B C D   4. The two most common gases in the earth's atmosphere are oxygen and (A. carbon; B. neon; C. nitrogen; D. hydrogen).

T F   5. Pneumatic means "lung."

A B   6. Davy took care of the large family debt by (A. declaring bankruptcy; B. paying it back).

T F   7. Davy kept secret most of his discoveries.

T F   8. Humphry Davy used laughing gas during a hospital operation.

A B   9. James Simpson experimented with ether and had (A. great success; B. limited success).

         A B   10. Chloroform does not explode and has a (A. foul odor; B. sweet smell).

         T F   11. James Simpson became the personal physician to Queen Victoria.

Chapter Nine

Morton Defeats the Pain of Surgery

William Thomas Green Morton wanted to be a doctor. As the son of a penniless New England farmer he couldn't afford medical studies. Instead he took a course to be a dentist. In 1844 he settled in Boston with his bride, Elizabeth. She was 18 years old.

"I've not given up on a medical degree," he told her. "First I'll make enough money to build a house for you. Then I'll study medicine, too."

Right away William Morton earned a good income. He designed a set of false teeth much better than any then in use. His dentures required patients to have all of their old teeth taken out. The prospect of such a dreadful experience scared away some of his paying customers.

"If only I could pull teeth painlessly," William Morton

SYMPTOMS

1. Dentistry...a painful experience.

2. Sulfuric ether was ineffective because some patients would wake up during surgery.

3. Sulfuric ether had an offensive odor and caused some patients to have trouble breathing.

Can You Diagnose the Discoveries?

said. "I would become the richest dentist in Boston, perhaps in the entire world. But I've investigated and nothing is suitable."

"What are you going to do?" his wife, Elizabeth, asked.

"Well," he hesitated. "If you could wait a bit longer for that beautiful house and fine clothes. . . ."

"Of course I can," she said.

"Then I'll attend medical school to learn how to relieve pain," Morton said. Quickly he added, "I'll keep my dentistry practice, too."

Morton couldn't wait for the fall term to begin. He wanted to get a head start on his studies. "I'll hire a doctor to be my tutor," Morton decided.

He became the private medical student of Dr. Charles Jackson of Somerset Street. Dr. Jackson was one of the most colorful figures in Boston. He dressed as a dandy, attended parties in extravagant homes, and was a chemist, world traveler, and physician. He was also a non-stop talker. How the man talked! He could carry on an intelligent discussion about any subject under the sun.

Dr. Jackson's mind bubbled with ideas. Before he became the master of one subject, he jumped to another one.

William Thomas Green Morton started out as a dentist looking for a painless way to pull teeth. He soon set out to ease the screams of pain during surgery.

Right now he was loudly proclaiming to the world that it was he, Dr. Charles T. Jackson, who had invented the telegraph.

"I explained the whole idea to Samuel Morse during an ocean voyage," Jackson charged. "Why, Morse is merely a portrait painter."

Of course, a half-baked idea and a completed invention are entirely different. The conceited Jackson, however, wouldn't accept the difference. He claimed a half-dozen other ideas, too.

The fact remained: few men in the world knew so much about as many different subjects as Jackson. William Morton learned a lot from Dr. Jackson.

In the fall of 1844, William Morton entered the Harvard Medical School. One day he was led into the operating theater of the Massachusetts General Hospital to watch an amputation. While the surgery was being performed, the screams of the poor victim echoed in the operating theater. Some of the students watched stone-faced. Others turned away their eyes in horror.

Until then William Morton had wanted a way to pull teeth painlessly to make money. This put a whole new light on the matter. He set his sights higher. He'd rid operating rooms of the screams of helpless patients.

After reading all he could on the subject, ether stood out as the likely candidate. Ether is a light, flammable liquid that evaporates easily. In the late 1820s, Michael Faraday, Davy's assistant, inhaled small amounts of the vapor and reported the effect.

Yet, William Morton had already experimented with ether. The gas didn't seem to work.

"I'll try it one more time," William Morton decided. He brought up a rubber bag to hold the liquid. "First, I'll see what Dr. Jackson thinks of the idea."

At first, William Morton tried to keep his researches secret. Slowly, he led Dr. Jackson around to a discussion of gases that might deaden pain.

"Ether will do the job," Dr. Jackson said. He recited all the known facts about ether.

"I tried ether once," William Morton admitted, "but it didn't seem to work."

"You must use the pure diethyl ether," Dr. Jackson told him. "Buy it from Joseph Burnett. His apothecary is the only one that sells the pure grade."

Dr. Jackson examined the rubber bag.

Charles Jackson was a very intelligent man and tutor of William Morton. He claimed that he and not Morton was the inventor of the ether inhaler. He found there's a vast difference between talking about and completing an invention.

"This will never do. Ether eats right through rubber. Here, let me fix you up. Take this glass jar with a sponge in it."

William Morton purchased the ether from Burnett's. He tried it out first on his pet dog. After putting the animal to sleep, he pricked it with a needle. The animal did not move. Moments later the dog awoke, perfectly healthy. For 18 months William Morton tested ether on animals.

Then he tested it on himself. He locked the door, seated himself in the dentist chair, and soaked a hand-kerchief with ether. He noticed the time and breathed deeply through the handkerchief.

Suddenly he awoke. Once again he checked the time. "I was out for eight minutes," William Morton observed. "Now I must try it on a patient."

Late on the evening of September 30, 1846, Morton heard a pounding on his door. By the light streaming through the window, Morton saw the swollen and bandaged face of Eben Frost.

"Dr. Morton," Mr. Frost moaned. "You'll have to pull this tooth. I can't stand the pain of it any longer."

William Morton examined the man's swollen jaw. "Yes, the tooth will have to come out. I'll pull it at once."

When the patient saw the pliers for yanking the tooth, he fell back. "No . . ." he winced. "Oh, I can't bear the toothache or stand the pain of having it pulled. What am I going to do?"

William Morton comforted the man. "If you are willing, I have something that will put you into a kind of sleep. You'll not feel the extraction at all."

Wordlessly, Eben Frost nodded. He took the chair. William gave him ether to inhale. Soon the man fell asleep.

William Morton grasped the tooth firmly. The tooth held. He strained at the effort. Morton pulled harder. The patient didn't even stir.

Less than a minute later the patient groaned and blinked his eyes open. He braced himself. "Well . . . when will you begin?"

"It's out," William Morton said. He showed the man the abscessed tooth held in the pliers.

The excited patient confessed, "I didn't feel a thing!"

That night William told Elizabeth about the experiment. The idea horrified her. "If he'd have died you'd be put in prison."

"He didn't die," Morton pointed out. "Besides, I tested it first on myself."

Early in October, William went to Dr. John Warren's home. As head of Massachusetts General Hospital, he was the most respected surgeon in the United States.

William Morton pleaded for the opportunity to demonstrate painless surgery.

"Such preparations have been tried before," Dr. John Warren pointed out.

"None worked." The doctor's stern face softened. Almost in a whisper he added, "Painless surgery is every doctor's dream. I've almost given up hope. Is it possible?"

William Morton rushed ahead. "This will work, I'm certain of it."

Now Dr. Warren had to make a difficult choice. The test would be carried out on one of his patients. If the patient died, he would have to answer the critics. A lifetime reputation would be wiped out. It was an awesome choice. Dr. Warren nodded. "We'll give it a try."

They set the date for Friday, October 16, 1846.

William Morton continued to improve his methods. He believed the glass inhaler would work better if it had two openings. He took it to an instrument maker for the changes.

The night before the trial, William Morton could hardly sleep. He arose early Friday morning to pick up the new inhaler. The instrument maker didn't have it ready. William, in a fever of impatience, waited for the final touches to be put on the inhaler.

Precisely at 10:00 Dr. Warren strode into the operating room. Onlookers had already gathered. Students, doctors, and staff members jammed into every seat. The patient, a pale and rather frightened Gilbert Abbott, waited. He seemed resigned to whatever fate awaited him.

The spectators grew restless.

Several blocks away, William Morton was beside himself with impatience. The instrument maker still fiddled with the ether inhaler.

Five minutes passed. Back at the operating room, the crowd began to whisper and laugh. Dr. Warren motioned for silence. "We'll wait for Dr. Morton."

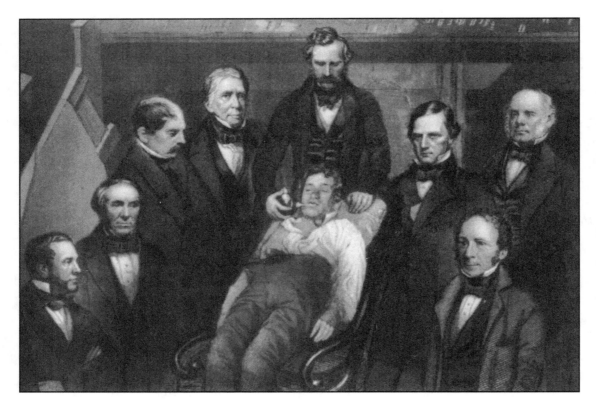

Morton demonstrates the use of diethyl ether at Massachusetts General Hospital. As Dr. Morton administered the vapor, the patient fell into a deep sleep. All those around watched to see if he would feel any pain.

The instrument maker held up the glass globe to examine it. Morton plucked it from his hands and raced along the streets toward the hospital.

Dr. Warren looked at the clock. Fifteen minutes after ten. The delay irritated him. *Morton has probably backed out*, the surgeon thought to himself. Aloud he said, "As Dr. Morton has not arrived, I presume he is otherwise engaged." He couldn't keep the sarcasm out of his voice.

As the spectators laughed, William Morton burst into the operating theater. Puffing and out of breath, William Morton explained the delay. "I need a few minutes longer to charge the inhaler."

Morton prepared the inhaler. He mixed some perfume with the ether, both to disguise its well-known odor and also to make it easier for the patient to breathe.

Suddenly, Morton was terribly nervous. What if the patient struggled and fought with the doctor? What if the patient shrieked and tried to jump up? The students would laugh. The doctors would nod knowingly. Catcalls and cries of "Humbug!" would bombard his ears. William Morton would be disgraced. He'd never be given a second chance.

The patient was strapped in a heavily padded operating chair. The operation would go ahead whether the painkiller worked or not.

Morton began to administer the vapor. The patient shuddered a little, and fell into a deep sleep. William Morton stepped back, bowed to the surgeon and said, "Your patient is ready, doctor."

Dr. Warren took the scalpel and with the speed of a master surgeon cut away the growth. The patient did not stir as the blade cut into his flesh. The doctor sewed up the wound and wiped away the blood.

The patient stirred. He awoke. "Did you feel any pain?" Dr. Warren asked him. The theater grew silent. The viewers leaned forward, listening for the reply.

The young man spoke in a shaky voice. "No, it didn't hurt at all."

Dr. Warren turned to face the silent crowd. He called out, "Gentlemen, this is not humbug!"

The news of Morton's success spread rapidly. Within two years doctors throughout the United States and Europe adopted anesthetics. They became more bold in operating procedures.

Do you think William Morton was satisfied to be one of the great founders of modern medicine? That turned out not to be the case.

William Morton's moment of triumph was tempered by the fact that he was penniless. His long-suffering Elizabeth had allowed him to pour everything into his pursuit of the painkiller. William Morton patented his discovery. It was so simple any doctor could duplicate the procedure. Many did.

Disaster of another sort struck. Dr. Charles T. Jackson came forward and claimed full credit for the discovery. He engaged in a vicious public battle with Morton over the discovery. Jackson pointed out that he'd experimented with ether first and instructed Morton in its use.

Morton tried to answer the claims. They fought the matter out in medical journals and in the press. The quarrel so enraged Morton, he abandoned his dentistry practice. For the rest of his life, Morton spent his time, energy, and every penny he could scrape together supporting his claim as the discoverer of ether as an anesthetic.

England offered Morton a generous prize for his discovery. Dr. Jackson raised such a ruckus

Today, a modern anesthetist must be a doctor especially trained in anesthetics. When the doctor is sure the patient is asleep he still repeats William Morton's words: "Your patient is ready, doctor."

that they withdrew the offer. The French Academy of Medicine offered a similar prize, provided both men shared it. Morton refused, rather than let Jackson have any of the money. Because of their jealousy, each man prevented the other from receiving any money.

Actually, neither man had been the first to use ether for surgery. That honor went to Crawford W. Long, a Georgia doctor. He had used ether in 1842 while removing a tumor from the neck of a patient. He repeated the experiment eight more times, but he didn't publicize his methods until 1849. By then he was only one of many who claimed to have put ether to use for surgery.

In medicine and science, credit is given to the one who perfects an idea and tells others about it, not to the one who has the idea first.

Who deserved credit for the discovery of painless surgery? The Massachusetts General Hospital appointed a commission to investigate the matter.

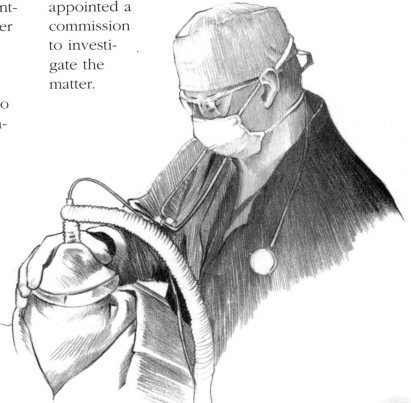

Most of the members of the commission knew Jackson personally. It appeared he would win the case. But the commission ruled that Morton, not Jackson, should be given the credit for painless surgery.

The commission's ruling didn't settle the controversy. In July 1868, while riding in a carriage, William Morton happened upon a newspaper account favorable to Jackson. Morton's face grew scarlet. He crumpled the paper in anger. Suddenly, he fell unconscious. William Morton suffered a stroke and never recovered. He died a few days later.

Elizabeth, his wife, summed it up. "The greatest personal tragedy in my husband's life was his discovery of ether."

Ironically, his enemy, Jackson, suffered a similar fate. One day he walked through a cemetery in Boston and came across Morton's tombstone:

William C. G. Morton
Inventor of anesthetic inhalation.

Savage jealousy struck Jackson again. All of his life insanity had lingered just below the surface. This time something in his mind snapped. He read the inscription and went completely mad.

They found Jackson in the cemetery, raving at the tombstone. They carried him off to the McLean Asylum. He remained there, completely insane, until his death in 1880.

The two men became terrible examples of how personal pride can ruin a person's life. Likely both Morton and Jackson would have gone on to other discoveries if they had devoted their energies to research rather than controversy.

Despite the conflicting claims, one point became clear to the world. The use of ether in surgery was completely American in its origin. The discovery marked one of the first times that the new country had made a major medical breakthrough.

Even an American invented the term "anesthetic." Oliver Wendell Holmes, an American author and physician, is better known today as the author of *Old Ironsides* and *The Wonderful One-Hoss Shay*. He was a skilled Boston doctor and the dean of Harvard's Medical School. He suggested the term "anesthetic" for a chemical that renders a person insensitive to pain. He based that name upon a Greek word meaning "no feeling."

The invention of surgical anesthesia is one of the key discoveries of modern medicine. Today, an anesthetic may be given only by a doctor who has special training in its use. Once the patient is asleep, the anesthetist repeats the words first spoken by William Morton: "Your patient is ready, doctor."

DIAGNOSES

1. William Morton invented a special glass inhaler and added perfume to ether.

2. Morton successfully used ether to pull a tooth and to then perform painless surgery.

3. Dr. Charles Jackson gave Morton some advice on using ether and then later claimed that it was all his idea.

Answer T or F for true or false, or
Select A — D for the phrase that best completes the sentence.

T F   1. William Morton earned a good income as a dentist.

A B C D   2. William Morton attended medical school (A. as a favor to his wife; B. to become a better dentist; C. to become a doctor; D. to learn how to relieve pain).

A B   3. Before his medical studies began, William Morton received private instruction from (A. Charles Jackson; B. Oliver Wendell Holmes).

A B   4. Charles Jackson claimed he had invented the (A. steamship; B. telegraph).

T F   5. William Morton learned nothing useful from Dr. Jackson.

A B C D   6. William Morton tried either first on (A. a patient; B. himself; C. his pet dog; D. his wife).

A B C   7. The one who was late to the first public demonstration of ether was (A. the surgeon; B. the patient; C. William Morton).

A B C   8. The first person to use ether in surgery was (A. William Morton; B. Charles Jackson; C. Crawford W. Long).

A B   9. William Morton suffered a stroke after (A. winning a prize for his accomplishment; B. reading a newspaper account favorable to Jackson).

A B   10. Charles Jackson became insane after (A. seeing the inscription on Morton's tombstone; B. reading that William Morton won a prize).

T F   11. The word anesthetic means "no feeling."

Write the letter of the matching choice.

12. _____ said, "No, it didn't hurt at all."

13. _____ said, "Gentlemen, this is no humbug!"

14. _____ said, "Your patient is ready, doctor."

15. _____ coined the word anesthetic.

A. Dr. Warren, a surgeon at Massachusetts General Hospital
B. Gilbert Abbott, a patient at the Massachusetts General Hospital
C. Oliver Wendell Holmes
D. William Morton

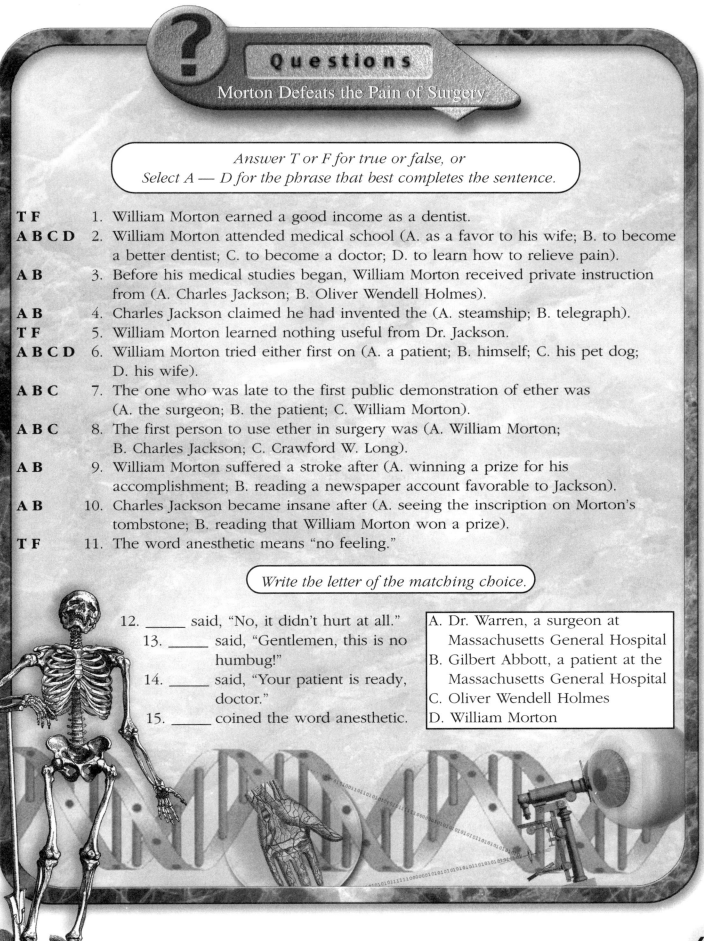

Death House in Vienna

Ignaz Philipp Semmelweiss (pronounced ZEM-el-vise) attended the University of Vienna, Austria, to study law. A friend, Jacob Kolletschka, invited him to attend a lecture on medicine. Saving lives seemed more worthwhile than winning lawsuits, so Philipp changed his studies to become a doctor.

In 1844, Semmelweiss graduated from medical school. He immediately accepted a position as assistant director of the Vienna Maternity Hospital. His boss was Director Johann Klein, a stern and overbearing man. Poor women came to the maternity hospital to have their babies. "They are charity cases," Director Klein pointed out, "and cannot pay. We must save money wherever we can."

SYMPTOMS

1. Childbed fever was taking thousands of lives of young mothers.

2. More women were dying under the care of doctors than midwives.

3. Some doctors were more interested in their reputations than in saving lives.

Can You Diagnose the Discoveries?

The hospital had two wards: one to train doctors, the other to train midwives. Semmelweiss was an obstetrician, a doctor who takes care of women during childbirth. An older practice, mentioned in the Bible, is for specially trained people, known as midwives, to help in births.

Expectant mothers who entered the hospital were sent to one of two wards — one run by the midwives, the other by doctors. For some reason, women begged to be sent to the midwife's ward.

"Whatever for?" Philipp asked one anxious patient. "Surely you'd prefer to be treated by a doctor than a midwife."

Sobbing, the woman shook her head. She wouldn't give Dr. Semmelweiss her reason. Clearly, she was afraid to speak, thinking she might offend him. From others, he heard the rumor that women feared the doctor's ward because more patients died there than in the midwife's ward.

Although Director Klein objected, Philipp Semmelweiss began investigating the hospital conditions. Each ward held

Ignaz Philipp Semmelweiss attended the University of Vienna, Austria. While there, he changed from law to medicine because he wanted to save lives. He became an obstetrician and discovered that doctors seemed to be spreading childbed fever to the young mothers.

about 400 patients. In one ward, where only the midwives worked, about 4 or 5 mothers died each month. To Philipp's dismay, in the second ward, where doctors attended the mothers, as many as 100 patients died each month — 1 mother out of 4!

Philipp Semmelweiss talked it over with his friend, Jacob Kolletschka.

"Is it really that bad?" Jacob Kolletschka asked. He taught at the maternity hospital, too.

"The death rate in the doctor's ward is appalling," Philipp said. "I've collected the facts. Director Klein wasn't too happy to give them out. I can understand why. In the last six years about two thousand women have died in the doctor's ward.

"What about the midwife's ward?" Jacob asked.

"They suffered only seven hundred deaths."

Jacob couldn't believe it. "Your figures must be wrong."

Semmelweiss sadly shook his head. "No, my figures are entirely correct. The

doctor's ward is nothing more than a murder chamber. Ignorant midwives save more lives than trained doctors. Incredible!"

During his student days Semmelweiss had become interested in childbed fever. It was a type of infection, and the greatest killer of mothers at the maternity hospital. At the time he had thought of it as a scientific puzzle. Now that he saw the disease firsthand, he couldn't think of the problem in such unemotional terms.

Philipp Semmelweiss dreaded making his rounds at the doctor's ward. He dreaded the desperate moans of dying women and the frightened faces of their neighbors. Philipp patted their hands and tried to reassure them.

What could one person do to save the lives of all these helpless women? Dr. Semmelweiss became determined to track

A group of women are visiting a local maternity hospital. They are talking with the midwives instead of the doctors because the death rate in those wards are much lower.

down the cause of the childbed fever. A year passed. During that time he learned nothing to prevent the disease or even to reduce its deadly toll. Like so many doctors before him, he assumed childbed fever could not be spread by contact.

After a year at the hospital, Philipp took a vacation. When he returned he heard some terrible news.

"Jacob Kolletschka is dead," he was told. "Your friend became sick with some sort of blood poisoning, and within a week he died."

After the personal loss of the tragedy had softened, Philipp began to question the cause of his friend's death. What kind of blood poisoning? he wondered.

Philipp read the report of Kolletschka's death. "Why, the symptoms are those of childbed fever. Yet Jacob is certainly not a mother. How could a man get the disease?"

Then someone remembered an injury Jacob Kolletschka had received only a week before his death. "Kolletschka and a student were in the morgue, performing an autopsy on a woman who died of childbed fever. The student accidentally nicked Kolletschka's finger. It bled a little — only a few drops."

With cold logic, Semmelweiss saw the answer. He concluded that childbed fever was contagious. A contagious disease is one that can be transmitted on contact. His friend Jacob had acquired the disease from the corpse.

Dr. Kolletschka, the other professors and their students had been spending hours examining dead bodies. They would then proceed to their wards to attend to living, healthy patients.

Not only that, but the doctors didn't bother with cleanliness. A doctor might leave the morgue after dissecting a corpse, rush to the operating room for surgery, and then go straight to the wards. During this time he neither washed his hands nor changed his bloodstained coat. Young doctors actually prided themselves upon their blood-encrusted examination coats. It made them feel more experienced.

Philipp could not shake the horrible thought of his discovery. The doctors themselves were carrying the disease from

A woman is giving birth with the help of three midwives. The newborn baby is being cared for on the table. Midwives attended women who could not afford to pay the doctors in the hospital wards. They were known to take more care in cleanliness than the doctors.

dead bodies in the morgue to living patients, and then from one patient to the next.

The midwives performed no autopsies. Also, Philipp Semmelweiss knew that the head midwife demanded that the midwives be clean and neat. She even had her students line up each morning and hold out their hands, proving their fingernails to be clean. He still didn't know what caused childbed fever, but now he certainly knew how to prevent it: have the doctors wash their hands before examining patients.

That very day Philipp announced the discovery to his medical students.

The students looked at one another, confused and rather angry. They stared back at him coldly. "Wash our hands? We'll be humiliated."

Philipp looked at them confused. "Humiliated? In what way?"

Dr. Semmelweiss insisted that his students were to wash their hands in soap and water and then rinse in chlorine water. Unfortunately, the other doctors would not follow this practice. Because of the doctor's pride and disregard of Dr. Semmelweiss' findings, many women continued to die.

"Why, the head midwife has the midwives line up and present their hands to her each morning." The doctor puffed up his chest. "We're doctors, not midwives. We don't have time for such foolishness!"

"It's undignified!" another student said.

"I'm ashamed of you," Semmelweiss told his students. "To think you'd rather a poor mother die than lose your dignity. Incredible! Wash — wash or leave the hospital!"

When Professor Klein saw the wash basins, he immediately called for Philipp. "What's the meaning of this?" he demanded.

Philipp explained. "My students are to

wash their hands in soap and water and then rinse in chlorine water. It will prevent the occurrence of childbed fever."

"That's the most outlandish idea I've ever heard. You must be joking."

"No," Philipp said. "I'm perfectly serious."

"Then you must have lost your senses," Professor Klein snapped. "This experiment has no medical value. We must watch the budget. There's no money in the budget for soap and chlorine water."

Somehow Philipp Semmelweiss found the money for the soap and chemicals. He also replaced the bed linens as soon as they became soiled.

The students resisted the changes. Johann Klein agreed with the students. He openly encouraged them. He judged the success of a doctor by whether he became wealthy, not by how many lives he saved.

Yet, Semmelweiss' plan worked. The death rate in his wards dropped spectacularly. In 1846 the doctor's ward had averaged a 10 percent death rate — 1 woman in 10 had died. With Philipp Semmelweiss' simple hand-washing plan, the number dropped to 1 percent — only 1 woman out of a hundred.

"Coincidence," Director Klein said coldly. "Nothing but coincidence. Epidemics come and epidemics go."

"You are accusing us of murder!" his students cried. They blamed epidemics of childbed fever on the weather, bad air, overcrowding, coincidence — everything but themselves.

This photograph from around 1890 is of a surgical operation that was performed by doctors in a maternity hospital. Because of Semmelweiss' work on cleanliness, the mother and baby have a much higher chance of survival.

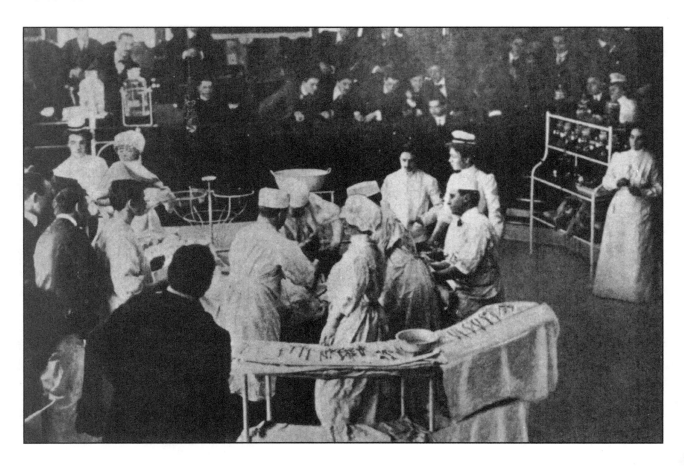

Then, in 1847, the death rate began to climb again. From one percent it rose to five percent. What could be the cause?

To Philipp's horror he found that young doctors deliberately disobeyed his orders! He hid out of sight. As he watched, a young doctor slipped in to see a patient. He hadn't washed his hands in the special chemical solution!

Philipp's cry of outrage stopped the student in his tracks. "You must positively wash your hands in the basin of chlorine water. No exceptions!"

The young doctor's face turned scarlet. "I'll have nothing else to do with this childish hand-washing in foul-smelling chemical solutions. Director Klein. . . ."

"You cold-blooded killer! OUT, out, and don't come back. You'll save more lives by leaving medicine than by becoming a doctor."

With Director Klein's backing, the students became more bold. They ridiculed Philipp Semmelweiss and ignored his teachings. And the poor young mothers continued to die.

Johann Klein looked for a way to punish Philipp. Finally Klein had his revenge. In 1849, Hungary and Austria went to war. Philipp was a Hungarian. Johann Klein used the war as an excuse to demote Philipp. He put Philipp in charge of teaching the midwives. Instead of treating an actual patient, he would train the midwives using a mannequin, a life-size doll.

Director Klein kept up the pressure and eventually drove Dr. Philipp Semmelweiss from Vienna. Philipp took a position at a hospital in Budapest, Hungary. As soon as he left, Director Klein tossed out the wash basins and poured out the chlorine water. The students rejoiced. Of course, with the end of hand-washing, the number of childbed fever cases climbed to record heights. Johann Klein and the medical students didn't mind. They were rid of the despised wash basins. That's what counted to them.

The Holy Bible, in the Old Testament Book of Leviticus, sets forth strict rules concerning contact with corpses, graves, and people with disease. For a time this seemed a strange idea to most people, even to doctors. How could cleanliness prevent disease?

Late in the 1860s, doctors finally began to accept the fact that many diseases are caused by tiny, microscopic organisms (germs), which could be spread from one person to another by contact.

The discovery of the germ theory of disease came too late for Ignaz Philipp Semmelweiss. In 1865 he nicked his hand while operating, and died of the same disease he had tried for so long to prevent.

DIAGNOSES

1. Dr. Phillip Semmelweiss discovered doctors were spreading childbed fever.

2. He proved that doctors were carrying the disease from corpses to their patients.

3. He proved that cleanliness could prevent childbed fever.

Answer T or F for true or false, or
Select A or B for the phrase that best completes the sentence.

A B 1. Semmelweiss decided to study medicine because he would
(A. earn more money; B. save lives).

A B 2. Director Johann Klein urged Semmelweiss to save (A. lives; B. money).

A B 3. The wards with the lowest death rates were those run by (A. doctors;
B. midwives).

A B 4. A contagious disease is one that a person
(A. inherits from his or her parents; B. acquires by contact).

T F 5. Jacob Kolletschka, Semmelweiss' friend, died of a disease he got from a corpse.

T F 6. The midwives prided themselves upon their bloodstained coats.

T F 7. The head midwife insisted the midwives have clean hands.

A B 8. When the doctors began washing their hands, the number of deaths
(A. decreased; B. increased).

A B 9. Deaths began going up again because the doctors
(A. did more autopsies; B. ignored Semmelweiss' rules).

T F 10. Philipp Semmelweiss died without learning about the germ theory
of disease.

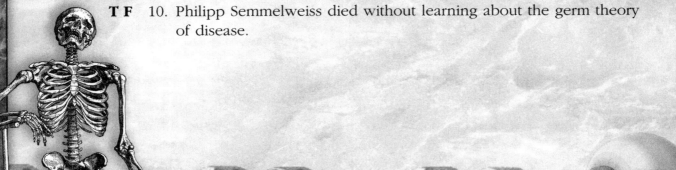

The Chemist Who Became a Doctor

Louis Pasteur, the son of a tanner of leather, lived in a small town in France. His father sacrificed to send him away for a better education. Louis became terribly homesick. "I must have a whiff of the tanyard," Louis wrote home. "I simply can't stay the full term." His kindhearted father let him come home for a time.

Louis Pasteur was a slow starter. He earned merely adequate grades. He didn't know what he wanted to do with his life. He toyed with the idea of becoming an artist. He almost finished college at Ecole Normale in Paris. Then he attended a lecture on chemistry. The speaker set Pasteur on fire for the subject. Louis threw himself into his studies. Nothing would stop him

SYMPTOMS

1. Could science be applied to practical matters?

2. It was difficult to ship food and wine because it often spoiled.

3. Doctors still did not understand how diseases were spread.

Can You Diagnose the Discoveries?

now. He lived on practically nothing, nearly starved himself, and drove himself on relentlessly. The "merely average" student mastered his subjects so well he could teach others. In that way he earned a little extra money. Incredibly, he managed to send money home to his parents.

His father could not have been more pleased with his son's turnaround. The elder Pasteur wrote to Louis and said, "Keep the money and spend it on yourself. My satisfaction in you is deeper than I can express."

By the time Louis graduated, he earned first prize in physics and honorable mention in three other subjects.

As part of his chemical studies, Louis Pasteur looked at tartrate crystals under a microscope. At first glance all of the crystals looked alike. Then Louis noticed a curious difference. The crystals were exactly like one another in every way except for being mirror images of each other, like left and right-handed gloves.

A well-known and respected chemist

Louis Pasteur had trouble deciding what he wanted to study until he was introduced to chemistry. There he found his life's work. Even though he was not a doctor, his contributions to medicine made him a great healer.

had flatly declared that he'd found no differences in tartrate crystals. Pasteur, an unknown, faced the difficult task of convincing others of the accuracy of his rather tedious experiment. Louis solved the problem by looking up an even better known and even more respected chemist, Jean Baptiste Biot.

"I have just made a great discovery," he told Biot. "I am shaking all over."

Before Biot's watchful eyes, Louis repeated the experiment. "The two tartrate molecules differ only in that one is a mirror image of the other."

Jean Baptiste Biot caught Pasteur's enthusiasm and helped him finish the experiment. He threw his support behind Louis who announced his discovery.

Later, Louis Pasteur made an even more remarkable discovery. Living things can tell the difference between a crystal and its mirror image. For example, glucose and galactose are made of 6 carbon atoms, 12 hydrogen atoms, and 6 oxygen atoms. Suppose you made a model of glucose and placed it in front of

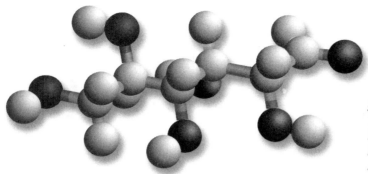

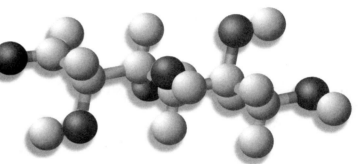

Pasteur discovered that some tartrate crystals have a mirrored image. The molecule on the left is glucose or common table sugar. The molecule below is its mirrored image, galactose. Soft drink companies use galactose in the making of diet drinks (below). The mirrored molecule fools the taste buds into tasting like sugar, but has fewer calories because the body does not digest it in the same way.

a mirror. The image in the mirror would be galactose.

The human body changes glucose to carbon dioxide and water. During the action energy is released. This energy powers the body's cells. Glucose is also known as blood sugar. Glucose can be used by the body. Galactose cannot be directly used.

Many food substances do exist in two mirror-image forms. If a person's diet were limited to the wrong ones, no matter how much he ate he would starve to death.

In recent years, chemists have found sugars that fool the taste buds but not the digestive system. A person can eat the sugar, enjoy the sugar taste, but the body doesn't digest it. Sugar-free sodas are sweetened with this mirror-image type of sugar.

In 1854, the town of Lille in the north of France decided to try an unusual experiment in learning. Businessmen in the area set aside money to begin a university. They invited Louis Pasteur to become the director of science. They warned him, "The

purpose of Lille University is to train young men in practical matters. Will you be willing to focus your teaching upon practical uses of science?"

Knowing that Pasteur spent his time in the laboratory, many people thought he would turn down the offer.

Instead, Louis jumped at the chance to teach at Lille. "It is an unusual idea," Louis agreed, "that ordinary businessmen should be trained in science, too. But science must earn its keep."

One day in the summer of 1856 a student brought his father to see Louis Pasteur. Monsieur Bigo, a distiller of alcohol, said, "My son studied in your laboratories. He thinks you may help with our problem."

"What is your problem?" Louis asked.

"Wine often goes sour as it ages," Monsieur Bigo said. "Wine spoils so soon after bottling it cannot be sold overseas. Millions of francs are lost because of it."

"I'll look into the matter," Louis promised. Here was his chance to show that science could solve real life problems.

Louis Pasteur turned his attention to the process of fermentation, the change of sugar into alcohol and carbon dioxide. Scientists at that time believed fermentation to be nothing but some sort of chemical action. It seemed reasonable that a chemist like Louis might discover how to prevent wines from going bad.

Louis had grown accustomed to using a microscope when he separated the left and right-handed tartrate crystals. It was natural to use the microscope in the study of fermentation. He examined samples taken from good wine and from wine that had gone sour.

In both samples he found yeast; some

Louis Pasteur studied samples of good wine and sour wine under a microscope and found that both contained yeast. He concluded that a round-shaped yeast (shown above) changes sugar to alcohol and that a second rod-like yeast changes alcohol to acetic acid, which is sour. To keep the wine from going sour, he decided to wait until the first yeast finished their work, and then gently heat the wine to kill the second yeast.

were little globes, others tiny rods. No one believed the little globes and rods to be alive. No one except Louis. He watched them under a microscope. "They are alive," he whispered. "They multiply. Fermentation is caused by living things."

Yeasts are single-celled organisms with a life of their own. Yeasts are a type of fungus. Like all fungi, yeasts have no chlorophyll so they cannot make food directly. Instead, they absorb food from the nutrients around them. Yeast breaks sugar down to alcohol and carbon dioxide.

Louis summarized his findings. "Two types of yeast grow in grape juice," Louis said. "The round ones change sugar to alcohol. A second rod-like yeast changes alcohol to acetic acid, which is sour. Round yeasts act first. When they finish their job, the second yeasts start working. The second yeasts cause wine to go bad."

"What can be done?" Monsieur Bigo asked.

Louis offered a solution. "The remedy is to wait until the first yeasts have finished, and then heat the wine gently, to about 120°F. This will kill the second yeasts so the wine does not go sour."

Monsieur Bigo drew back, aghast at such an idea. "Heat will destroy the taste!" he cried.

"No," Louis said. "The few minutes of heating will not change the flavor."

The winegrowers weren't convinced.

"We'll put it to a taste test," Louis said. He heated some kegs of wine and left others unheated. Samples were taken

from both kegs. The winegrowers themselves couldn't tell the difference.

Then the winegrowers loaded the kegs in the hold of a ship as if for export. Several months later they unloaded the kegs. They drew samples again. This time the taste had changed.

"Phew!" Monsieur Bigo said. "The wine in the unheated kegs has gone sour."

Of course, Louis Pasteur's process could also be used to protect milk and countless other beverages and foods. A new word entered the major languages of the world: pasteurization. It is the process of gentle heating to kill harmful microorganisms.

"This procedure will make you a wealthy man," Monsieur Bigo told Pasteur.

Louis Pasteur shook his head. "I have decided to release the patent to the public. That is why I came to Lille, to bring science to the benefit of mankind."

Pasteur wrote a report about his discovery of pasteurization. Thoughtfully,

This cartoon shows gentlemen going through the four stages of wine tasting to tell if the wine is good or not. The winegrowers were afraid that Louis Pasteur's solution of heating the wine to keep it from spoiling would destroy the wine's taste. When they put it to a test, the growers could not tell any difference between the heated and normal wine.

and without any real proof, he added a line: "Infectious disease might be caused by these micro-organisms."

Pasteur's study of yeast cells brought him to the question of how microscopic life arose. Most scientists believed some vital force brought microscopic life into existence out of non-living matter. The idea is called spontaneous generation. "Their numbers always increase when wine ferments, milk sours, or meat spoils," they explained. "Spoiling food causes them to spring into life."

According to this view, there was no point in studying microscopic life. The tiny microbes that mysteriously sprang into life one day would be totally unlike microbes that appeared the next day. A microbe is the name given to any living thing so small it can only be seen in a microscope. Microbe means "small life."

During the l700s, the great Carolus Linnaeus undertook the awesome task of classifying all living things. He grouped them according to similarities and differences. Linnaeus threw up his hands at the idea of studying the multitude of tiny living things seen through the microscope. "There are too many of them," he said, "and too difficult to observe."

The process of pasteurization is used in many products that we use today. For example, this jug of milk has been pasteurized (heated) to kill any bacteria or other organisms that would make it unsafe to drink.

Linnaeus lumped all microscopic life together and called them chaos, a word meaning "total confusion."

In 1859 Charles Darwin announced his theory of evolution. As a first step in that theory, life must arise from non-life — spontaneous generation.

Pasteur rejected the theory of evolution for scientific reasons. He was the first European scientist to do so. He also rejected it on religious grounds. He said, "There is something in the depths of our souls which tells us that the world may be more than a mere combination of events."

Louis didn't believe in spontaneous generation. "All living things must come from living things," he reasoned. "Only from microbes arise microbes."

"Where do microbes have their start?" scientists challenged him. "Take a flask," they said, "and fill it with meat broth. Boil the broth until all life in it is killed. Set it aside. Within a few days, the meat broth will teem with microbes. What can be their source except the broth itself?"

As a first step, Louis repeated the experiments of Lazzaro Spallanzani, an Italian biologist. In 1786, Spallanzani concluded that microbes appeared only because dust particles carrying them fell into meat broth. When he sealed flasks after boiling them, meat broth did not spoil. In fact, since the early 1800s people have preserved food by heating it and sealing it in cans and jars.

Those who believed in spontaneous generation objected to Spallanzani's methods. "The long heating destroyed the vital principle in the air," they said.

"Natural air must be allowed back into the flask after it is heated." Somehow Louis had to overcome the objections to Spallanzani's experiments. He talked it over with a friend, Professor Jerome Balard.

"I believe microbes cannot arise in the meat broth by themselves," Louis said, "They must fall in from the air."

Balard agreed. "Yes, so you must boil the broth, kill the microbes already there, but let natural air enter the flask."

Thoughtfully, Louis nodded. "But how?"

He solved the problem by making several bottles with long S-shaped necks. He heated the bottles and their contents to boiling and left them to cool. Air could freely flow into the

Louis Pasteur believed the microbes could not arise in the meat broth he was experimenting with by themselves. He used the S-shaped flask to prove his theory. He heated the bottles and their contents to boiling. Air could flow into the bottles but the S-shaped necks trapped the dust particles. The broth did not spoil. He proved that the broth could sit indefinitely without spoiling, even in the open air, as long as the dust did not reach it.

bottles, but the S-shaped necks trapped dust particles at the bottom of the curve.

The meat broth did not spoil. No decay took place. Louis examined a drop from the broth under a microscope. Not a single microbe appeared. Then he swirled the broth around, until it went up into the bend of the neck. The broth washed over the dust particles trapped there. Within days, the broth became cloudy from the millions of microbes growing within it.

"Micro-organisms drop out of the air," Louis said.

To drive home his point Louis Pasteur left the laboratory. He tested the air in dozens of places. He went into the cellars of the Observatory of Paris and to the high Alps. He opened bottles to the air. Where the air was clear and dustless, such as high in the Alps, his bottles of meat broth developed no life. In dirty air, the flasks filled with microbes.

In 1864, Louis Pasteur presented his findings before a scientific gathering in Paris. "Never will the doctrine of spontaneous generation recover from the mortal blow that this simple experiment has dealt it. There is no way for microbes to come into the world except from parents like themselves."

"Into that flask," Louis Pasteur told his audience, "I have put all the elements needed in the development of microscopic organisms. I have kept it from the only thing we do not know how to produce — life."

Some of the S-neck flasks that Louis prepared more than one hundred years ago can still be seen today in the Pasteur Institute in Paris. The fluid is as clear as the day Pasteur heated it. It is totally lifeless.

In 1865, the silk growers to the south of France came to Louis Pasteur and begged his help. "The silk industry is in shambles," they said. "A disease has struck silkworms and threatens to destroy us. The silkworms become sick before they change into a chrysalis."

"What's a chrysalis?" Louis asked.

They explained, "It's the living silkworm inside a cocoon. Silkworms have four stages in their lives: egg, worm-like larvae, chrysalis in the cocoon, and adult moth. The silkworm is a larvae. It is born from an egg laid by a moth. These worms live on mulberry leaves. Then they spin cocoons, which are unraveled to give silk threads.

"Our worms become sick and sluggish. They die before spinning their silk cocoon. The disease is dealing a staggering blow to our economy."

"Why come to me?" Louis asked. "You can see that I know nothing about silkworms."

"So much the better," the silkgrowers said. "You will have only those ideas which come to you as a result of your own observations."

A symptom of the disease was the appearance of black spots, like grains of pepper. Once again Louis Pasteur made use of the microscope. He found microorganisms growing in the pepper spots on the silkworms. The same microbes grew on mulberry leaves. The disease was passed along to the eggs, too.

Louis offered a drastic solution to the problem. "Burn the infected worms and leaves," he told the silk growers. "Once destroyed, you can start afresh with healthy silkworms and new mulberry bushes brought in from China."

It worked.

Silk growers asked Pasteur to find out why their silkworms were dying. Pasteur discovered by using his microscope that micro-organisms were growing not only on the pepper spots on the silkworms but also on the mulberry leaves. His solution was to burn the infected worms and leaves and start with healthy silkworms and new mulberry bushes. After they followed Pasteur's instructions, the silkworms were able to survive.

Louis Pasteur could not shake the thought: if microbes can cause disease in silkworms, then microbes might cause disease in humans, too.

Doctors violently disagreed. "Pasteur is a quack. We need no outsider to tell us how to run our affairs. Leave medicine in the hands of those who have been trained in healing!"

"Microbes are killers," Louis said. He begged doctors to steam their bandages, to boil their surgical instruments, to wash their hands before going from patient to patient. Such steps would kill microbes and prevent diseases.

Yet, because he held no medical degree, doctors ignored his pleas. "There is no connection between the death of silkworms and the diseases of people."

Louis Pasteur attended a medical meeting. A doctor talked about childbed fever. He described atmospheric conditions as the cause. Louis stood up and interrupted. "The cause of the epidemic is nothing of the kind. It is the doctor and his staff who carry the microbe from a sick woman to a healthy woman."

He went up to the blackboard and drew a picture of the microbe. "There! That is what it is like."

During his own lecture, Louis Pasteur turned on a lantern that sent a beam of light across the lecture hall. "Observe the thousands of dancing specks of dust in the path of this ray," he cried. "The air of this hall is filled with these specks of dust on which microbes are carried."

Pasteur's germ theory of disease was probably the single most important medical discovery of all time. It answered many questions that didn't have a solution otherwise. It explained the success of Dr. Semmelweiss in preventing infection.

Louis Pasteur received many honors from his native France. Some scientists resented his fame. They claimed his success was only the result of good luck.

"Good luck favors the prepared mind," Louis pointed out. One of the ways he prepared his mind was a devotion each morning. He read the Bible and prayed before going about each day's activity.

He'd already earned enough fame for a dozen people. He was probably the most dedicated scientist of all time. Well, why not? "Science is an enchantment," Louis Pasteur said. "It's not work when it is fun!"

Then at the crest of his fame, a tragedy struck. Louis suffered a stroke that paralyzed his left side. It threatened his life. He was 46 years old. Because of the stroke, most people believed his scientific career was over. Louis Pasteur would not allow tragedy to easily defeat him. We'll see how it turned out in a later chapter.

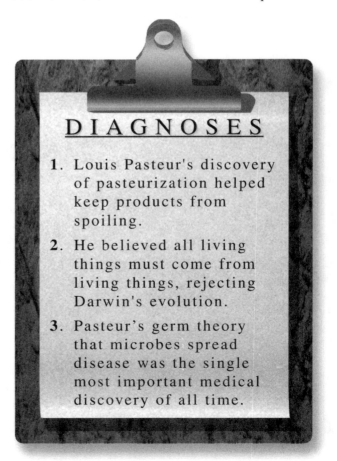

DIAGNOSES

1. Louis Pasteur's discovery of pasteurization helped keep products from spoiling.

2. He believed all living things must come from living things, rejecting Darwin's evolution.

3. Pasteur's germ theory that microbes spread disease was the single most important medical discovery of all time.

Answer T or F for true or false, or
Select A — D for the phrase that best completes the sentence.

A B   1. Louis Pasteur's grades at Ecole Normale in Paris improved after he attended (A. a medical demonstration; B. a lecture on chemistry).

T F   2. The only difference between galactose and glucose is that they are mirror images of one another.

A B   3. Louis Pasteur showed that fermentation is caused by (A. excessive heat; B. yeasts that are alive).

T F   4. Pasteurization is the process of air drying to kill harmful micro-organisms.

A B C D   5. Spontaneous generation is the belief that microscopic life can (A. cause fires; B. cause meat to spoil; C. come into existence out of non-living matter; D. spread from one generation to the next by infection).

T F   6. Louis Pasteur rejected the theory of evolution.

A B   7. Louis Pasteur proved that spontaneous generation (A. occurs in the high Alps; B. never occurs).

A B C   8. Louis Pasteur showed that silkworms became sick because of (A. bad air; B. microbes; C. poisoned leaves of mulberry bushes).

A B   9. When Louis Pasteur suggested that microbes could cause disease, doctors (A. rushed to test his idea; B. said, "Pasteur is a quack").

T F   10. Louis Pasteur prepared his mind by reading the Bible and praying each morning.

A B   11. When he was 46 years old, Louis Pasteur (A. suffered a stroke; B. made a fortune from pasteurization).

Joseph Lister Fights Infection

Joseph Lister, a freshman medical student, watched the first use of ether in England in December of 1846. He was a serious-minded young man, shy, and spoke with a bit of a stammer. Joseph's father warned him against becoming a surgeon. The father thought surgery would be too brutal for his kindhearted son.

Joseph Lister saw that ether took surgery into a new era. Anesthesia made all the difference. He wrote home. "I've decided to become a surgeon myself," he said, "if I prove to have the necessary skill."

Joseph Lister did have the skill. After earning his medical degree he took a position at the Glasgow, Scotland, hospital. Despite the success of

SYMPTOMS

1. Infection was a major problem during surgery.

2. People often died after surgery from the infection alone.

3. Compound bone fractures almost always ended in death because of infections.

Can You Diagnose the Discoveries?

anesthesia, surgery still terrified patients, and with good reason. Doctors ignored Pasteur's germ theory of disease, just as they'd ignored Semmelweiss. Patients still died after surgery, not of pain or shock, but from infection due to unclean conditions in the hospitals.

One man came to Dr. Lister to have a mole removed from his face as a favor for his bride. The operation was simple. Three days later, however, infection set in. The man died.

Joseph Lister asked, "What is the use of operating on a patient if he is to die of infection?"

He checked the hospital records. In Joseph's own hospital, about two in five surgery patients died. In Paris, about three in five. Munich, Germany, held the grim record — four in five of the cases there ended in death. City officials threatened to burn the hospital if conditions didn't improve.

Joseph Lister, a serious-minded young man, was thought too kindhearted by his father to be a good surgeon. His compassion drove Lister to find a better way to combat infections that took so many lives. He is now remembered as one of the greatest of surgeons.

Older doctors still quoted Galen: "Infection is useful. The pus cleans the wound and helps healing." If wounds didn't develop infection naturally, doctors applied rough dressing to cause pus to appear.

Joseph Lister looked for a better answer. An important clue came from his treatment of broken bones. Glasgow was an industrial town. The city's machinery sent its share of broken bones and mangled bodies to the hospital for treatment. Fractures (broken bones) were of two types: simple and compound.

A simple fracture was one in which the leg or arm broke, but the bone didn't come through the skin. A simple fracture could be set and would heal without difficulty. Patients with simple fractures seldom developed a fever. No infection set in. Usually, the patient fully recovered.

A compound fracture was one in which the broken bone cut through the flesh and was exposed to the air. Despite Lister's best efforts, the place where the bones stuck out of the skin got red. The wound began to develop an unpleasant odor. The patient ran a fever. Finally, in more than half of the cases the patient died.

Broken bones of the compound type posed a terrible danger to the patient. Time and again, Joseph Lister watched the

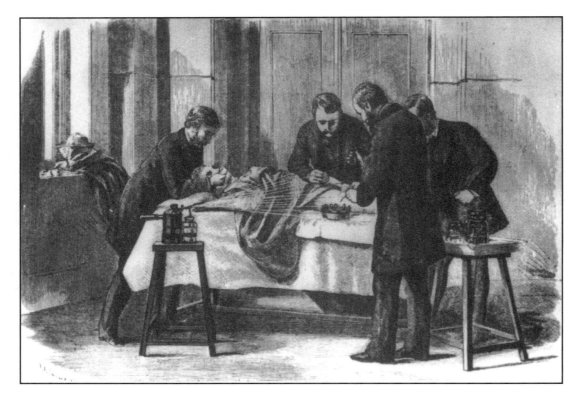

would kill the patient, too. Maybe a chemical would stop them. Any suggestions?"

"Carbolic acid may work," his friend said. "The Germans use it when sewers start to smell."

Joseph asked, "An acid?"

Professor Anderson explained, "Unlike sulfuric acid, carbolic acid is very weak. It may be strong enough to kill germs, yet not be so strong as to damage the flesh around the wound."

Joseph Lister experimented with a sample of carbolic acid. He sniffed it and drew back. Although it smelled terrible, he decided to try it on the next compound fracture that came into his ward. He didn't have long to wait. A boy named James Greenless was admitted to the hospital. A heavy wagon had run over the boy and had broken his leg. The bone protruded through the flesh.

Joseph Lister painted the edges of the wound and the protruding splinters of bone with carbolic acid. Then he set the bone, dressed the wound with a piece of cloth dipped in carbolic acid, and bound the leg.

terrible cycle: redness, swelling, infection, pus, fever, and finally death. How could he break the cycle?

He talked it over with Professor Thomas Anderson, a friend and chemist. Joseph asked, "If the fracture is a compound one, so that the bone pokes through the flesh, the patient is unlikely to recover. Why the difference?"

Professor Anderson told Dr. Lister about Louis Pasteur. "Pasteur is not a medical doctor at all; he is a chemist like myself. He believes that tiny living things in the air can drop into an open wound. He claims these tiny germs are the cause of disease."

"He may be right," Joseph Lister agreed. "Simple fractures heal because the broken bone isn't exposed to germs in the air."

Professor Anderson said, "Pasteur has developed a way to stop the growth of germs by heating them."

"I can't heat the patient until the germs die," Joseph Lister said. "That

Joseph Lister cared for the boy personally. When at last he took off the bandages, a scab covered the wound. The leg healed normally. His patient left the hospital with his leg as good as new.

"He recovered as if it had been a simple fracture," Joseph Lister said.

He continued to look for ways to avoid germs. Most doctors washed their hands after a surgical operation. Joseph Lister washed his hands before going to the operating room. Most doctors wore dirty "operating" coats with dried blood on them. Joseph Lister, on the other hand, wore a clean linen apron. He became the first white-robed doctor.

Doctors used silk string to sew up incisions. They carried short lengths of string looped through the buttonholes of their coats. When they needed to tie an artery or sew up a wound, they simply pulled one of these threads out of their buttonholes and used it. Often the flesh around the stitching became infected. Joseph Lister noticed this. He soaked his threads in carbolic acid before using them.

The hospital made bandages and dressings of worn-out sheets, towels, and tablecloths donated by members of church groups. Most hospitals did nothing before using them. They didn't even wash the bandages before putting them on wounds. Joseph Lister insisted upon more soap, clean towels, and washed bandages. The board of governors who ran the hospital grumbled at the expense.

They believed it to be a waste of money.

Joseph kept everything clean. He washed surgical instruments, the operating table, his hands, and the patient. The results astonished him. Surgery became much safer. His record of patients who survived was unbelievable. In fact, some doctors simply didn't believe him. They called him a liar.

Joseph Lister learned to ignore the controversy. His personality radiated peace and love. He visited his patients daily and changed their bandages himself. Most surgeons employed assistants known as dressers to do this work. Joseph Lister asked his patients if he could do anything to make them more comfortable.

Once, he came into the wards to find an eight-year-old girl crying. "Here, what's the matter?" he asked the girl. Gently, he sat on the edge of the bed beside her.

The girl stopped sniffling. "Nurse took away my doll."

The nurse explained, "The doll has a torn leg. Sawdust is leaking out." Joseph Lister took the doll and gravely sewed up the leg. He treated the doll with as much care as his human patients. The girl got well, and so did her doll.

Even kind-hearted gestures like this drew fire from critics. "You are setting a bad example," they said. "Doctors must be held in awe and respect by their patients."

At age 50, Joseph Lister moved to King's College

Dr. Joseph Lawrence developed a disinfectant for surgery, which was not too harsh on human skin. It was manufactured and sold by Jordan Wheat Lambert (the Lambert in the Lambert-Warner Company) for use in the home. They called it Listerine in honor of Joseph Lister.

Hospital in London. The London doctors openly resented his successful surgery. For a time, they refused to send nurses to help him in the operating room.

Joseph Lister, a Christian, had a gentle nature, an even temper, a determined will, and an unselfish character. He overlooked the harsh words. He said, "My results speak for themselves."

By 1875, Joseph Lister had won over the rest of the world. German doctors in Munich put his methods to work. Joseph Lister toured Europe and saw in person the change at the Munich hospital. Its dismal record of 4 deaths out of every 5 patients had improved to less than 1 death in 200 patients.

The German doctors didn't use carbolic acid. Instead, German surgeons boiled instruments and sponges to be used in operations. Joseph agreed to try it himself. "It is not the presence of acid that matters," he said, "but the absence of germs."

Dr. Lister's discovery became known as antiseptic surgery. The word antiseptic is the combination of "anti" meaning "against" and "septic" from a Greek word meaning "to make rotten." An antiseptic prevented the growth of the germs that attacked human flesh.

Carbolic acid was not entirely satisfactory to use as a disinfectant. Its action was too harsh on human flesh. Chemists took up the challenge and discovered solutions less irritating to human tissues and even more deadly to germs.

Dr. Joseph Lawrence developed a disinfectant that could be used during operations without damaging human tissue. Later, it was manufactured and sold by Jordan Wheat Lambert and William R. Warner as an effective mouthwash. They named it in honor of Joseph Lister.

They called it Listerine.

At last doctors couldn't deny that Joseph Lister had been right. Hospitals became sparkling clean places.

Joseph Lister outlived his critics. He became a hero. During the last 30 years of his life (he died in 1912 at age 84) he enjoyed immense respect. A grateful world showered honors upon him. He became the first physician to belong to the House of Lords, part of the British Parliament. Scientists elected him president of the Royal Society. He became physician to the Queen of England.

Today Dr. Joseph Lister is considered the greatest surgeon of all time. Like so many other great scientists who were also Christians, he was a humble and gracious man.

The combined work of Leeuwenhoek, Semmelweiss, Pasteur, and Lister established that germs cause disease and that keeping germs from entering the body prevents infection. This discovery is one of the top ten medical discoveries.

DIAGNOSES

1. Joseph Lister discovered that carbolic acid prevented infection on compound fractures.

2. By insisting that everything be kept clean and disinfected, he lowered the death rate in his surgeries.

3. He discovered it was not the presence of acid but the absence of germs that mattered in surgery.

Answer T or F for true or false, or
Select A — D for the phrase that best completes the sentence.

T F   1. Death from infection was so common in Munich, Germany, that city officials threatened to burn the hospital.

T F   2. Some doctors actually encouraged infection to develop.

A B C D   3. A compound fracture is one in which (A. a bone breaks in more than one place; B. more than one bone breaks; C. a broken bone cuts through the flesh; D. a patient breaks the same bone a second time).

A B   4. The one that healed without complication was a (A. compound; B. simple) fracture.

T F   5. Louis Pasteur claimed that tiny germs caused disease.

A B   6. Carbolic acid is (A. stronger than sulfuric acid; B. very weak).

A B   7. When Dr. Lister learned that German doctors boiled instruments to kill germs instead of using carbolic acid he (A. opposed the idea; B. agreed to try it himself).

T F   8. Antiseptic means against smell.

T F   9. Listerine is named after Joseph Lister.

A B C D   10. Joseph Lister became (A. the first physician to belong to the House of Lords; B. president of the Royal Society; C. physician to the Queen; D. all three).

The Search for Disease Germs

Robert Koch dreamed of being an explorer. He grew up during the age of exploration. The source of the Nile River had not yet been found. Africa was still an uncharted continent. In the Pacific, mysterious islands waited to be discovered. Ships on voyages of discovery took along a doctor. Robert Koch decided to become a doctor. Then he would join a sailing expedition. That way he could voyage to faraway places with strange-sounding names.

His life did not follow the course he'd plotted for it. He fell in love and gave up those dreams to be with the woman he married. Even so, he remained restless and moved from one small town in Germany to another. He ended up as a poor country doctor in the province of Posen.

SYMPTOMS

1. Epidemics of anthrax were killing cattle, sheep, and sometimes humans.

2. Farmers had to kill, burn, or bury the animals to prevent the spread of anthrax.

3. The disease would still re-occur.

Can You Diagnose the Discoveries?

Robert Koch did get to explore a whole new world. By some miracle of thrift, his wife saved enough money to buy him a new microscope. She gave it to him as a birthday present. At first, Robert Koch played with the microscope like a little child with a new toy. He spent hours looking at the world of the infinitely small.

While he grew skilled at using the microscope, an epidemic struck a nearby farming community. From ancient times herds of animals had died from a mysterious illness called anthrax. It is known in the Bible as murrain, one of the plagues upon Egypt.

Anthrax was a frightful disease. Usually it killed livestock like cattle and sheep, although humans died from it, too. It could strike suddenly. A sheep would be perfectly healthy one day. The next day the farmer would find the animal cold and stiff, its blood turned a horrible black.

Veterinarians (animal doctors) had no cure for the disease. When anthrax struck, farmers had to kill the animals and burn them or bury them deep, otherwise the disease came back the next year.

Robert Koch wanted to be an explorer but when his wife gave him a microscope, he began a great exploration of the microscopic world. This journey would lead to the discovery of what had eluded doctors for centuries — the cause of the killer disease anthrax.

Why were such drastic measures necessary?

Robert Koch decided to study anthrax. Why not? He'd been looking for an excuse to spend even more time with his microscope.

He'd need a laboratory. He called a carpenter to put a partition across the room where he met patients. But he couldn't wait for the carpenter. He hung a sheet to curtain off one corner of the room. There he set up his equipment. Except for the microscope, his laboratory contained no professional equipment. Instead, he made what he needed or put common household utensils into use. He used kitchen plates as laboratory glassware.

He looked through his microscope at blood of animals dead from anthrax. Time after time he noticed strings of living bacteria in the shape of rods. Bacteria are tiny, one-celled oraganisms. They come in many different shapes and sizes. Like yeast, bacteria contain no chlorophyll. Koch found none of these particular rod-like bacteria in the blood of healthy animals.

This illustration from the late 1800s is titled "The Latest Contribution to the Germ Theory." A bacteriologist is sitting at a table with jars of bacteria from deadly diseases that he has been studying with his microscope. Most people at that time thought it ridiculous that diseases could be caused by germs so small as to be invisible to the unaided eyes. To show how unbelievable the germ theory seemed, the cartoonist has the scientist writing down his discovery as told to him by a tiny imaginary angel.

Robert Koch read the medical journals. Within their pages, the controversy raged concerning germs. Could these tiny bacteria really cause disease? If they did, how could he prove it?

First, he would have to find a way to grow bacteria outside the body so he could follow their life cycle. With an oil lamp and a box he made a crude heater to keep the bacteria at body temperature. He discovered that the bacteria would grow in the clear fluid from the eye of an ox.

He transferred some of the blood to a drop of the fluid. By morning the drop swarmed with rod-like bacteria. The few bacteria of the night before had grown to thousands.

Now for the next step. Would the bacteria in the fluid cause anthrax in healthy animals?

He couldn't give the disease to sheep. He was a poor country doctor. Sheep cost too much to be used as experimental animals. Then he thought of mice. They would be ideal. He put a wire screen along the front of a bookcase and turned it into cages for his mice. Patients who came to his office were greeted by the smell of disinfectants and the sound of mice scurrying.

He took a mouse, cut a small slit in the skin above its tail, dipped a sliver of wood in the fluid that swarmed with the bacteria, and inserted it under the mouse's skin. The next morning he found the mouse on its back dead, its body stiff, and its blood black.

He transferred the disease from mouse to mouse. All mice diseased with anthrax always carried the same rod-like bacteria in their blood. When he injected the bacteria into healthy mice, they came down with anthrax, too.

One day he watched as the drop of

fluid holding the bacteria began to dry up. As it did, the bacteria changed into little beads. Robert Koch called these bead-like objects spores. They resisted heat, light, and cold. Yet the spores were as deadly as the bacteria.

These spores explained why farmers had to take such extraordinary steps to rid their farms of anthrax. When conditions turned against anthrax bacteria, they drew themselves into tough spores. The spores could survive freezing winters and hot, dry summers. Only a tiny spark of life kept burning within them. The soil held the spores, waiting for new victims. When animals ate them, the spores sprang back into life and did their deadly business.

Simply killing infected cattle wasn't enough. The bodies had to be burned or buried deep enough to put the spores out of harm's way. Robert Koch had solved the mystery of anthrax. He could point to this particular type of bacteria and say, "Here is the cause of anthrax." He smiled shyly to himself. Should he announce his discovery? No, not yet. He wanted to try a few more experiments.

Robert Koch now set himself to the task of photographing the bacteria. He saved enough money to buy a camera. The old-fashioned glass negatives he used needed strong,

bright light. He devised a series of mirrors to reflect sunlight through a hole in the window to the microscope.

The bacteria were small, nearly transparent, and hard to see. Then Koch discovered dyes would stain bacteria. Different bacteria seemed to react to different colors. After he found the right dye, the very smallest microbe stood out clearly. Photographs he took remained the best for more than 50 years.

One day Robert noticed half of a boiled potato that had been left, quite by accident, overnight in his laboratory. Little colored spots were scattered on the flat surface where it had been cut in half. He examined material from the colored spots through his microscope. Each spot proved to be a pure colony of a particular bacteria. During the night, bacteria had fallen upon the potato surface. Where each one landed, there it stuck, and there it multiplied — a colony formed of millions of bacteria, all alike.

In liquids, different kinds of bacteria put on the surface of a liquid mix easily. They are impossible

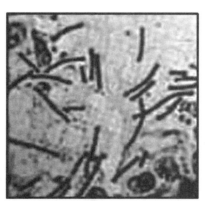

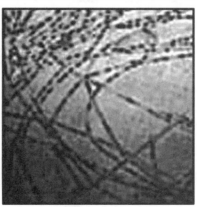

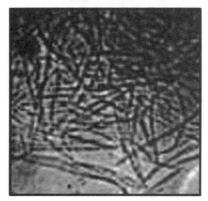

These photographs taken by Koch show the deadly rod-shaped bacteria that causes anthrax. Using fluid from the eye of an ox, he found that he could grow the bacteria outside the body to study them.

to keep separate. On solids, bacteria cannot move about. Each one stays rooted in its spot and gives rise to a patch of millions of identical germs. Robert Koch could grow pure strains of germs by starting them on the surface of a solid.

Later Robert Koch learned even a better medium, or culture, for growing germs. He mixed gelatin with beef broth, to give a solid surface.

Now it was time to tell the world about his discovery. Robert Koch lived far from a major medical school. At that time (and even now), scientists listen to those who work at well-known universities. Who would listen?

He wrote Professor Ferdinand Cohn at the University of Breslau and begged to be given a hearing. After checking Robert Koch's claims, Ferdinand Cohn gave Robert Koch three days at the university to present his discovery.

It was one of the strangest demonstrations of all time. Robert Koch didn't lecture. Instead, he repeated his experiments, showing with microscope and photographs exactly what happened. Robert Koch handled the equipment with the cool confidence of a seasoned professional. He never doubted the outcome. Spores formed, bacteria grew, mice died. What a show!

Each day began with more excitement and a larger crowd. On the third day, professors dismissed their classes. They told their students, "Go and watch the country doctor!"

Robert Koch set down four simple rules to find which bacteria causes a particular disease: One, find the suspect bacteria in sick animals. Two, grow the germ by itself outside the body. Three, inject the bacteria into a healthy animal. Four,

the newly infected animal must come down with the disease and yield bacteria of the same sort as found in the original animal.

Although the professors at the university considered Koch an outsider, his experiments overwhelmed their objections. Even the great Louis Pasteur himself had never been so thorough.

At the conclusion of the three-day event, Robert Koch asked for questions. There were none. He'd left no room for doubt. From that day in 1876, no one seriously doubted the germ theory of disease.

Robert Koch proved that each disease is caused by a particular bacterium. These infinitely small animals could kill a sheep or ox — or human. Although Robert Koch had shown the cause of anthrax, he'd not found a cure for it. Smallpox was still the only disease that could be prevented by vaccination.

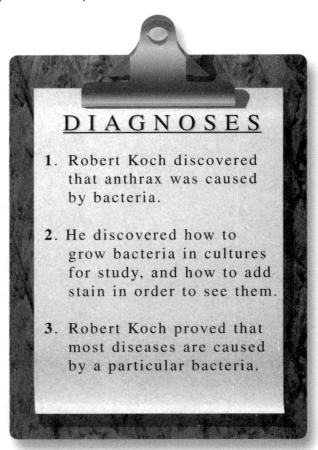

DIAGNOSES

1. Robert Koch discovered that anthrax was caused by bacteria.

2. He discovered how to grow bacteria in cultures for study, and how to add stain in order to see them.

3. Robert Koch proved that most diseases are caused by a particular bacteria.

Answer T or F for true or false, or
Select A — D for the phrase that best completes the sentence.

A B C D 1. Robert Koch dreamed of being (A. a candlestick maker; B. doctor; C. explorer; D. lawyer).

A B C 2. Robert Koch received a microscope as a gift from his (A. children; B. father; C. wife).

A B C D 3. To rid their livestock of anthrax, farmers had to (A. feed them oats; B. give them shots; C. keep them in the barn; D. kill them and burn or bury them).

T F 4. Robert Koch worked on the problem of anthrax in a well-equipped research laboratory.

T F 5. Spores carried a mild form of anthrax.

A B C 6. Robert Koch's photographs (A. had little scientific value; B. remained the best for more than 50 years; C. were lighted using flash powder).

T F 7. When bacteria grow on a solid surface they grow in colonies in which the bacteria are all alike.

A B 8. At the university, Robert Koch proved his ideas by three days of (A. experiments; B. intense lectures).

A B 9. On the third day of Robert Koch's demonstration, the professors told their students (A. go and watch the country doctor; B. stay away from this man).

T F 10. Robert Koch proved what caused anthrax, but did not find a cure for it.

Louis Pasteur Again

When we last left Pasteur, he'd found the microbes that soured wines and killed silkworms. The dedicated chemist suffered the tragedy of a stroke which left him paralyzed and in danger of death. After a week he was out of danger, but his doctors said he'd never walk again. Many people assumed his scientific career to be over. Actually, however, his greatest and most important medical discoveries were yet to come.

He rallied from his illness. A week after the attack, he was sitting up in bed and dictating a letter. His body might not have been fully working, but there was nothing wrong with his mind. In three months he returned to his laboratory. "Go here," he told his assistants. "Do that!" Soon he

SYMPTOMS

1. During an epidemic of cholera, a farmer could lose as many as 11 out of every 12 chickens.

2. No cure for the disease anthrax had been found.

3. The disease of rabies always proved fatal.

Can You Diagnose the Discoveries?

was the center of a swirl of activity as if he'd never been away.

What can explain his recovery? It's likely that part of the answer was his own fighting spirit. He maintained a spiritual strength that helped him overcome physical limitations.

Even so, the stroke did leave its mark upon him. It caused permanent paralysis of the left arm and leg. Yet he learned to walk with no more aid than that of a cane.

His wife, Marie, figured in his recovery, too. In fact, she figured in all that he did. Soon after his graduation from Ecole Normale, Pasteur had married Marie Laurent. Marie realized she had married a genius. She provided an ideal home life for him. She put his work ahead of everything else. She let him handle scientific problems. All of the other numerous details of running the house she took onto herself. She did it all, she said, "So he might retain the full freedom of his mind for his investigations."

In turn, Louis Pasteur always found time each year for a vacation in the country with his wife. He put away his microscope and notebook. For two weeks he devoted himself completely to her happiness.

As sometimes happens between a loving husband and wife, they became a devoted team. Their lives intertwined. It is difficult to know where the accomplishments of one end and those of the other begin.

Louis Pasteur in his laboratory before his stroke. Although Pasteur later suffered paralysis of his right arm and leg in a stroke, it did not stop his relentless search for the cure of diseases.

She listened as he explained his experiments. She wrote out his notes. She asked him to explain his ideas to her. By explaining them to her, the ideas became clearer in his own mind. Louis Pasteur learned to express himself so ordinary people could understand. When scientists refused to accept his breakthroughs in medicine (and they did) he could go beyond them and enlist public support.

Pasteur next tackled chicken cholera, a highly contagious disease of fowl. When the disease struck, chickens became listless. They would go to roost, their drooping heads sunk into their ruffled feathers. Then they died. During an epidemic, a farmer would be fortunate if 1 in 12 of his chickens lived.

Pasteur found the bacteria responsible and grew them in chicken broth. A drop

of the broth on a crumb of bread proved quickly fatal to the healthiest hen. So he had found the culprit, and he knew how to keep the bacteria alive. But how could he prevent the disease?

The solution came quite by accident. Pasteur closed down the research lab for his yearly vacation. Upon his return, two of his assistants gave chickens some of the infected broth. But they drew the sample from an old bottle that had been put aside while Pasteur was away. Somehow the bottle got mixed up with the new ones.

The chickens sickened but did not die. By next morning they seemed perfectly well again. The assistants discovered their mistake. They apologized to Pasteur. "We didn't notice the date on the label."

Pasteur waved aside their explanation. He could sense that he was onto something. "The old bacteria gave the chickens a mild case of cholera," Pasteur said. "What will happen if we give the same chickens a dose of fresh, strong cholera bacteria?"

They took a new, vicious culture and injected the same hens with it. To everyone's utter astonishment, the chickens didn't become sick at all.

Then Pasteur made one of the leaps of imagination only he seemed capable of making. "Don't you see," he cried. "These birds have been vaccinated!"

Just as vaccination with cowpox protected a person from smallpox, so vaccination with weakened cholera bacteria protected chickens from cholera. By being exposed to a weakened form of the same bacteria, they became immune to it. Jenner had named his discovery vaccination, basing the word upon the Latin word for cow. Although Louis Pasteur's discovery had nothing to do with cows or cowpox, he kept the name "vaccination" in honor of Jenner's discovery.

Now he knew how to combat disease bacteria: just vaccinate the animal with weakened bacteria of the same disease.

"It turns bacteria against themselves!" Louis Pasteur cried. "We'll go after anthrax next."

Pasteur read the published reports of Robert Koch's experiments. Robert Koch, a German, had identified the bacteria that caused anthrax. Very well, Pasteur would develop a vaccination to prevent the disease!

How could Pasteur conquer anthrax? He had discovered the mild form of chicken cholera by accident. Now he set out on purpose to discover a mild form of anthrax. It was the first time that anyone dared to develop a vaccination for a specific disease.

"There is no weak form of anthrax," one of his assistants pointed out.

"We'll make one," Louis Pasteur said, "by heating anthrax bacteria, or aging them, or treating them with chemicals."

After many experiments, success came by controlled heating of deadly anthrax bacteria. Choosing the right temperature took expert skill. Too warm and the germs multiplied and stayed as strong as ever. Too cool and they changed into the nearly lifeless spores. At exactly the right temperature, the bacteria grew old and weak.

The vaccine worked! Louis Pasteur announced the wonderful news. Once again he found himself involved in a bitter quarrel. Veterinarians, doctors who take care of animals, had watched helplessly as anthrax took its toll. Now they refused to believe that a mere chemist could have solved the problem that had baffled them for so many years.

Rossignol, a famous veterinarian, edited a magazine called the *Veterinary Press*. All the veterinarians and farmers who raised sheep and cattle read the magazine. Rossignol thought Pasteur to be a fraud. He demanded a field test. He surely believed that Pasteur would refuse. He hoped to embarrass Pasteur before the whole world.

Louis replied, "I am delighted to accept the challenge. What has succeeded in the laboratory will succeed on the farm."

On May 5, 1882, at a farm near Melun, France, farmers herded 50 sheep into a pen. The public test began. To half of the sheep Pasteur gave shots of weakened anthrax. The other 25 would be the control. To those he did nothing. Then on the last day of May, he injected all 50 sheep with a very powerful and dangerous strain of anthrax bacteria.

Newspapers carried a day by day account of the experiment. The suspense grew. All of France waited for the next news.

"How many will survive?" a reporter asked.

Louis expressed complete confidence. "All of the control sheep will die. All of the vaccinated ones will live."

"All?" the reporter asked.

"Yes, all. The ones I treated must live or you can tell your readers the experiment failed!"

Maybe Louis showed more confidence in public than he actually felt in private. He took the train back to Paris. There he waited out the results. On June 2, after a sleepless night, the doorbell rang. A telegraph arrived. Pasteur's hands shook so badly he couldn't open the envelope.

Marie tore open the envelope. She read the telegraph to him. "Sick sheep among vaccinated lot all completely recovered. Unvaccinated sheep all dead or dying. Stunning success."

Rossignol himself had sent the telegraph. Louis Pasteur could claim complete victory.

No longer would farmers have to kill their livestock, burn them, or bury them deep when anthrax struck. Instead, they could vaccinate against the disease. Cattle could even graze in complete safety on infected pasture land.

Because the anthrax test had been held in public, it was a public triumph. Louis Pasteur's discovery became the talk of all Europe. He returned to the laboratory to take aim at another disease. He had gotten the victory over diseases of silkworms, chickens, and livestock. Now he took on rabies — a human disease caused by the bite of a mad dog.

People feared rabies for the very good reason that the disease always proved fatal. A person bitten by a mad dog didn't always get the disease. Those who did sometimes didn't become ill for several days. Once the symptoms developed, there was no hope. In all of history up to

Pasteur knew that controlled heating of the anthrax bacteria would cause it to grow old and weak. Now came the time for the public test. On May 5, 1882, 50 sheep were herded into a pen. To 25 sheep Pasteur gave shots of weakened anthrax. The other 25 were given nothing. Then on the last day of May, Pasteur injected all 50 sheep with a very powerful strain of anthrax bacteria. On June 2, a telegraph arrived telling Pasteur, "Sick sheep among vaccinated lot completely recovered. Unvaccinated sheep all dead or dying. Stunning success."

Pasteur's time, not a single person had survived once the disease had made its appearance.

The signs of a dog with rabies could not be mistaken: the half-opened mouth, froth covered jaws, bloodshot eyes, and despairing howls. The disease attacked the dog's nervous system. A dog drinks water by lapping it up with his tongue. Once rabies strikes, a dog cannot control his tongue. The poor animal becomes terribly thirsty, yet is unable to drink. Merely the sight of water sends the pitiful animal into a frenzy of torment. For that reason people had named the disease hydrophobia, meaning "fear of water."

Imagine Louis Pasteur working only inches from the snapping jaws of these struggling ferocious animals. Louis Pasteur, himself partially lame and over 60 years old, took samples of the foam from the mouths of these snarling animals.

Louis became convinced that the nervous system was the home of the agent that caused rabies. This explained why several weeks might pass before a person came down with the disease. Although rabies germs might enter the body from bites to the arms or legs, they must make their way to the brain and grow there.

Patiently he followed the steps that had spelled success so many times before: find the germ, figure out a way to grow it outside the body, and develop a weakened form.

Louis could not find the germ. Today we know why. Rabies is caused not by bacteria but by an agent much smaller — a virus. A virus is a bit of living crystal, so small it cannot be seen by ordinary microscopes. It can only be seen with powerful electron microscopes.

Louis could not grow it outside the body. A virus must grow within a living cell. So attempts to keep it alive in a culture such as chicken broth, as Pasteur had with cholera, were doomed to failure. Instead, he had to grow the virus in living animals. He chose rabbits as the host. When one rabbit died, he transferred the disease to another one.

Next Louis Pasteur and his assistants searched for a way to weaken the virus. Success finally came by removing the spinal cord of a rabbit that had died of rabies. They hung the spinal cord by a thread in a clean jar and

kept the material hot and dry. After 14 days, rabies lost its strength.

Now Louis Pasteur faced a problem of another sort. Domestic animals, like the family pet dog, could carry rabies. So could wolves, skunks, bats, and other wild animals. Pasteur couldn't go around vaccinating all these animals. Even if he

This illustration is of Pasteur's experiments with hydrophobia. The signs of a dog with rabies could not be mistaken: Half-opened mouth, froth-covered jaws, bloodshot eyes, and despairing howls. The dog could not control his tongue and could not drink. The sight of water sent the animal into a frenzy of torment. For that reason, people had named the disease hydrophobia, meaning "fear of water."

Pasteur is removing the spinal cord of a rabbit who had died from rabies. He found that rabies was caused not from bacteria but from a virus. He found by hanging the spinal cord in a jar and keeping the material hot and dry for 14 days the virus weakened and could now be used as a vaccine for humans.

did invent a vaccine for rabies, what good would it do?

We'll not vaccinate animals before they get the disease," Pasteur said. "We'll vaccinate the human victim after he has been bitten."

Louis Pasteur reasoned, "Rabies attacks slowly. A vaccine given after a bite can still produce immunity in time to save the victim's life."

It would be a race against time — Pasteur's vaccine against the spreading rabies virus. How long could a person wait after being bitten to begin the anti-rabies treatment? No one knew.

"We must make many more tests before we dare use it on human patients," Pasteur told his assistants.

Before the series of tests could be conducted, a mother brought her little boy, Joseph Meister, to see Louis. On his way to school the nine-year-old boy had been attacked by a mad dog. The animal had badly mauled him. Deep gashes covered his body. The wounds alone had nearly killed him.

The mother explained, "Our doctor heard of your work. 'Take your son to Paris at once,' the doctor told me. 'Take him to Louis Pasteur.' "

"My remedy is untried and possibly dangerous," Louis Pasteur told the woman. "I'm not ready to try it on a human being."

"My son is doomed anyway," she pointed out.

With gentle hands, Louis Pasteur examined the brave little boy. Why, the gashes were so deep he could hardly walk.

Still, Louis Pasteur hesitated. This would be his first human patient. He simply couldn't take action without seeking expert medical opinion. He took the boy to two doctors, members of the Rabies Commission in Paris. They examined the boy in detail. Finally, that evening the doctors gave their verdict. "The boy will certainly die if nothing is done."

On July 7, 1885, 60 hours after the attack, Louis Pasteur began the treatment. One of his assistants, a doctor, vaccinated the boy. Louis Pasteur could not do it himself because he was not licensed to practice medicine.

They began with the material weakened by drying for 14 days. This they followed with 12 more injections, each one stronger than the one before.

During the ten days of the treatment, Pasteur could not work. He sat by the little boy's bed. He ate little and slept hardly at all. When he did sleep, he dreamed that Joseph Meister was dying a horrible, suffocating death as rabies took over.

Marie Pasteur wrote, "My dear children, your father has had another bad night. He is dreading the last inoculations on the child. And yet there can be no drawing back now."

Finally, on July 16, they injected material from the spinal cord of a rabbit that had died of rabies only the day before. It contained the full-strength virus. Even if the mad dog hadn't given Joseph Meister rabies, the last injection would probably give it to him anyway.

As the days passed, Joseph Meister showed no ill effects.

Louis dared to believe in success. "Very good news last night of the bitten lad. It will be 31 days tomorrow since he was bitten."

The treatment worked. The boy never developed rabies. He returned home, completely untouched by the disease. Joseph Meister became the first human being to escape the certain death of rabies. Newspapers worldwide reported Louis Pasteur's defeat of rabies. Many desperate victims of mad dog attacks poured into Paris to seek help. Their numbers overwhelmed Pasteur and his assistants.

The people of France set up an organization to handle the cases. They started to collect money to build Louis Pasteur a new research laboratory. The people of the world would not let France be the only one to honor Louis. Donations came from America, from the czar of Russia, the emperor of Brazil, the sultan of Turkey,

Louis Pasteur is watching anxiously as a doctor injects Joseph Meister, who had been bitten by a rabid dog, with the first vaccine for rabies. Pasteur had to wait 31 long days before he knew the vaccine had been successful.

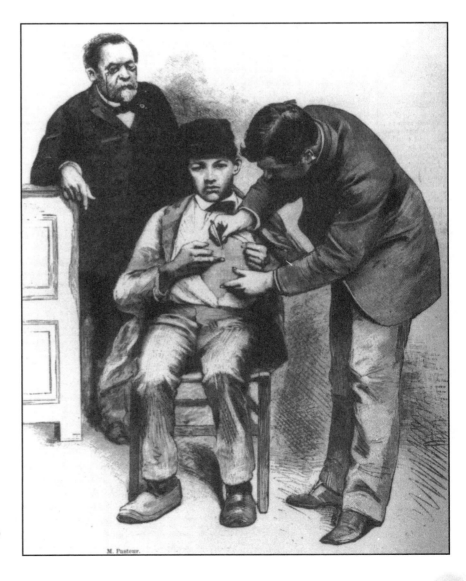

On December 27, 1892, Pasteur was honored by France and representatives of many foreign countries on his 70th birthday. Joseph Lister, the first to put his germ theory into practice, was there to honor him.

and from many other countries. The Pasteur Institute opened its doors on November 14, 1888. During his earlier days, one of Pasteur's laboratories was under some stairs going to the attic. Pasteur entered by getting on his hands and knees and crawling into the room. Those days were certainly behind him now. The Pasteur Institute took its place as the world's best-equipped medical research center. Joseph Meister, the boy whose life Pasteur had saved, grew up to become gatekeeper at the institute.

On December 27, 1892, government officials of France and representatives of many foreign countries gathered to honor Louis Pasteur on his 70th birthday. Dr. Joseph Lister had been the first to put Pasteur's germ theory into practice. He attended the celebration. He represented the Royal Society. Pasteur limped into the hall amid thunderous applause. Joseph Lister stood, walked forward, and shook

Pasteur's hand. The two great doctors embraced one another.

Although Pasteur never went to medical school, he is considered the greatest doctor of all time. Yet, those who met him without knowing him, did not guess that such a simple and humble man was the respected Louis Pasteur.

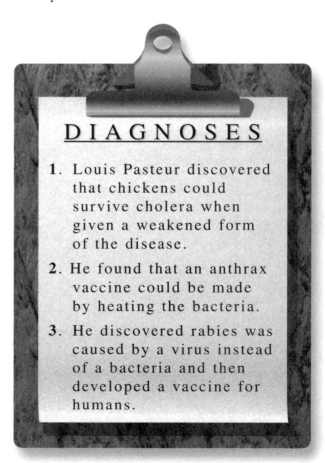

DIAGNOSES

1. Louis Pasteur discovered that chickens could survive cholera when given a weakened form of the disease.

2. He found that an anthrax vaccine could be made by heating the bacteria.

3. He discovered rabies was caused by a virus instead of a bacteria and then developed a vaccine for humans.

> *Answer T or F for true or false, or*
> *Select A — D for the phrase that best completes the sentence.*

T F 1. After Pasteur's stroke, many people assumed his scientific career to be over.

T F 2. Pasteur learned to get around in a specially equipped wheelchair.

T F 3. To combat disease bacteria, Pasteur learned to vaccinate an animal with a weakened bacteria of the same disease.

A B 4. Pasteur found the mild form of chicken cholera by (A. accident; B. a series of difficult experiments).

A B C D 5. Pasteur produced a weakened form of anthrax by (A. aging; B. controlled heating; C. freezing; D. chemically treating) the deadly anthrax bacteria.

T F 6. For the public test of anthrax to be a success, Louis Pasteur said all of the vaccinated animals must live.

A B 7. Rossignol described the results of the public test of anthrax vaccination as a (A. complete failure; B. stunning success).

T F 8. The number of people who survived rabies once the symptoms appeared numbered about a dozen each year.

T F 9. Rabies is also known as hydrophobia.

T F 10. Pasteur quickly found the rabies germ.

T F 11. Louis Pasteur succeeded in growing rabies germ in a potato culture.

T F 12. Louis Pasteur's treatment for rabies would begin after a human was bitten.

T F 13. Pasteur himself gave Joseph Meister the first injection against rabies.

T F 14. Pasteur never went to medical school.

Dr. Lind's Limes

In 1535, Jacques Cartier, the French navigator, anchored his ships along the St. Lawrence River. He spent the winter near the site that would later become Montreal, Canada. During the long, bleak winter more than a hundred men in his expedition came down with scurvy.

The word scurvy means "scaly skin." This disease causes its victims to lose weight and grow weak. Gums bleed and teeth loosen. Sores do not heal. Connective fibers weaken that hold the body together. Victims of scurvy die as if they have come apart.

Jacques Cartier's men did not die. The natives offered a homemade remedy: drink a tea of pine needles soaked in water. Despite the simple nature of the solution, the desperate sailors tried it. The Indian's tea brought them back to good health!

SYMPTOMS

1. Sailors were dying of scurvy.

2. The British Empire depended upon ships for commerce and national security.

3. Doctors failed to believe the Indian's homemade remedy of pine needles tea.

Can You Diagnose the Discoveries?

Doctors paid little attention to the Indians and their trial-and-error methods of curing disease.

A hundred years passed and scurvy remained the scourge of sailing ships. Sailors feared it like people on land feared smallpox. In the 1700s more sailors on British ships died of scurvy than of all other diseases, naval battles, and shipwrecks combined.

The British Empire depended on its ships for both commerce and national security. England is an island nation. The British took any threat to the smooth operation of the Royal Navy as a serious matter.

The problem of scurvy came to the attention of Dr. James Lind, a Scottish physician. In 1747 he began treating patients at the naval hospital in Edinburgh. Dr. Lind began his medical career as a surgeon's mate in the British Royal Navy. He was both shocked by the number of scurvy cases and disturbed because no one could cure it.

Dr. Lind read all about scurvy. It showed up not only on ships, but also in remote villages during long winters and on mountain-climbing expeditions.

During the age of sailing ships, sea voyages often lasted a year or more. These ships lacked a way to keep food from spoiling in its natural form. Instead, food was dried or preserved with salt. Fruits and vegetables were especially difficult to store and keep fresh. Sailors ate biscuits (hardtack) and salt pork.

For ten years Dr. Lind struggled with the problem. His studies began to point toward the lack of certain fresh foods, especially fruits and vegetables, as the cause of scurvy.

As an experiment, he selected 12 sailors who suffered from the disease. He divided the men into six pairs. Although he put them all on the same basic diet, he varied what they ate a little. To one pair he gave cider, to another spices, and so on. To one pair, he gave two oranges and one lemon every day.

At the end of a week, the two that ate oranges and lemons improved considerably. One returned to work; the other man stayed on and helped Dr. Lind with the experiment.

Dr. James Lind, a Scottish physician, began his medical career as a surgeon's mate in the British Navy. It was here that he began his search for the cause and cure of scurvy.

Captain James Cook, one of England's greatest sea captains, sailed for 4 years discovering the Pacific Ocean. His crew remained healthy because he followed Lind's advice and gave them citrus fruit.

Captain James Cook, one of England's greatest captains, learned of Dr. Lind's experiment. Captain Cook had made many voyages of discovery to the Pacific Ocean. He dreamed of a plan to explore the entire size and scope of the Pacific Ocean. It would take four years. To carry out the ambitious voyage would be a terrible burden to the crew under him.

"A large number of scurvy cases would almost certainly develop," Captain Cook explained to Dr. Lind. "Can you offer any help to prevent scurvy?"

"Yes, I can," Dr. Lind replied promptly. Like Captain Cook, Dr. Lind cared about the men. He proposed several changes: cleaner living quarters, professional medical help aboard ship, and plenty of fresh drinking water.

"Stock a wide selection of food," Dr. Lind told Captain Cook, "especially citric fruits such as oranges, lemons, and limes. During the voyage make landfall whenever possible to take on fresh food."

Captain Cook's voyage became one of the greatest sagas of all time. He sailed throughout the southern Pacific. He outlined the size of Australia, sailed around New Zealand, and plunged south to the ice and cold inside the Antarctic Circle. It took four years. He came home a firm believer in Dr. Lind's limes.

Unfortunately the British admiralty, the men in charge of the navy, did not take kindly to the suggestion that they'd been feeding British seamen poorly. They prided themselves upon having the best-fed and best-equipped navy in the world. They did put into practice Dr. Lind's other suggestions: hospital ships, clean quarters, fresh drinking water, and ventilators to bring fresh air below decks. They balked at supplying oranges and limes.

Ten years passed. Dr. Lind's success as a doctor grew greater. He became physician to King George II. He continued to

A young sailor is suffering from scurvy. The disease caused its victims to lose weight and weaken. Their gums would bleed and the sores on their bodies would not heal. The connective fibers would weaken that hold the body together. It was hard to believe that vitamin C, such a simple thing, could prevent and cure such a dreaded disease.

tell about his study of scurvy. Whenever captains of other vessels tried the citrus fruits, they, too, demanded fresh limes and oranges for their men.

In 1795 the admiralty finally gave in to progress. They reversed their stand. Now they ordered sailors to drink lime juice. Limes kept better than other citric fruit.

In the cartoon below, an injured sailor consults a quack doctor in the 1790s. The doctor insists upon payment before he will cure the sailor. This reflects the attitude that many had toward James Lind. They thought he had come up with a quack remedy to make money when he suggested a simple remedy for such a serious disease as scurvy.

In 1795 the British soldiers were finally ordered to drink lime juice. The limes kept better on the long voyages than other citrus fruit. The simple remedy wiped scurvy from British ships. It has caused British sailors to still be called "limeys."

The success of the program can be judged by the fact that to this day British sailors are called "limeys." The simple remedy wiped scurvy from British ships.

Neither Dr. Lind nor anyone else knew why citrus fruits saved lives. More than a century passed before doctors learned that scurvy is a dietary deficiency disease. It is caused by the lack of vitamin C in the diet.

In those days there was no refrigeration. The old-fashioned methods of preserving food — smoking, salting, drying — destroyed vitamin C. But fresh limes contain vitamin C. So do pine needles, which explains why the Indian remedy cured Jacques Cartier's men.

Although vitamin C is absolutely essential to good health, it need be present only in trace amounts. The total for the human body for an entire year comes to less than one ounce.

Despite Dr. Lind's victory over scurvy, most doctors of the 1800s refused to believe that a disease could be cured by simply eating the right food. In the 1870s, Louis Pasteur and Robert Koch proved the germ theory of disease. After that it became even more difficult to convince doctors to look to the diet to cure some diseases.

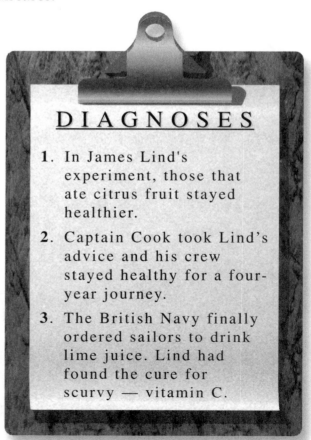

DIAGNOSES

1. In James Lind's experiment, those that ate citrus fruit stayed healthier.

2. Captain Cook took Lind's advice and his crew stayed healthy for a four-year journey.

3. The British Navy finally ordered sailors to drink lime juice. Lind had found the cure for scurvy — vitamin C.

Answer T or F for true or false, or
Select A or B for the phrase that best completes the sentence.

A B   1. Scurvy means (A. *I cannot*; B. *scaly skin*).

T F   2. Victims of scurvy die as if they have come apart.

A B   3. The greater killer of sailors on British ships was (A. *naval battles*; B. *scurvy*).

T F   4. The only suggestion Dr. Lind gave to Captain Cook was to carry limes for his men.

T F   5. Captain Cook's sea voyage lasted four years.

T F   6. Captain Cook returned home a firm believer in Dr. Lind's limes.

T F   7. Dr. Lind learned that citrus fruits save lives because they contain vitamin C.

Select the matching letter from the list below.

8. _____ had his men drank tea from pine needles soaked in water.

9. _____ treated sailors for scurvy in Edinburgh.

10. _____ explored the size and scope of the Pacific Ocean.

11. _____ balked at supplying oranges and limes for sailors.

12. _____ refused to believe that a disease could be cured by simply eating the right food.

13. _____ developed the germ theory of disease.

A. *The British admiralty*
B. *Captain James Cook*
C. *Dr. James Lind*
D. *Doctors of the 1800s*
E. *Jacques Cartier*
F. *Louis Pasteur and Robert Koch*

The Hidden Hunger

For many years during the 1800s the Dutch East India Company sent settlers to the Orient — to China, Java, and the beautiful islands of the Pacific. From the first, an unusual disease struck the settlers. The victims grew weak; they couldn't eat, their heart weakened, paralysis set in, and finally, death came.

Natives of the area called the disease beriberi. The word means "I cannot." Although for centuries a few local people suffered from the disease, it never became a major threat. For some reason beriberi struck the European settlers especially hard.

By 1885 officials of the Dutch East India Company spoke with Robert Koch. "Something must be done about beriberi," they said. "We need your help."

"I'd like nothing better than to go to the Orient to study the

SYMPTOMS

1. European settlers sent by the Dutch East India Company were dying of disease.

2. Victims couldn't eat, their heart weakened, then paralysis and death.

3. Because doctors thought germs caused all diseases, they were overlooking the role of the diet in health.

Can You Diagnose the Discoveries?

problem," he said. "Alas, the press of work keeps me at home. I cannot take on additional assignments."

"Whom do you suggest in your stead?" the officials asked.

"There is a former student of mine who would be perfect," Robert Koch said. "His name is Christiaan Eijkman."

The Dutch East Indies Company did select Christiaan Eijkman (pronounced IKE-mahn) as one of the members of the medical team. He was Dutch himself, living in Amsterdam, Holland. In 1886 they sent the young doctor to Java to tackle beriberi.

Only ten years earlier Louis Pasteur and Robert Koch had published their studies of how bacteria cause certain diseases. The germ explanation for disease led to triumph after triumph. Its victories caused most doctors to jump to the conclusion that germs of one type or another caused all diseases!

"All we have to do," Christiaan Eijkman said, "is find the germ that causes beriberi and destroy it." He worked on the problem at a hospital at Java. Beriberi patients filled the hospital wards. They had expert medical attention, clean bed

Christiaan Eijkman, a student of Robert Koch, was sent to the Orient to find the cause and cure of the disease beriberi.

sheets, and the "best" food — fluffy white rice.

Natives who lived outside the Dutch stockade knew little about modern medicine. They lived in unsanitary conditions and ate poorly processed food such as brown rice. Many diseases struck the natives — but not beriberi. Why?

Christiaan Eijkman desperately searched for the disease germ. He peered through his microscope at the patient's blood, the water they drank, the food they ate. The distress of the men stricken by the disease left him sick with worry. He couldn't find the germ.

The other doctors gave up. They left Java and sailed back home to Holland. Christiaan Eijkman refused to give up.

With money running low, he decided to inject chickens with blood from a beriberi patient. He performed the experiment and waited for the symptoms to show up in chickens. The chickens remained perfectly healthy. Perhaps the beriberi bacteria did not infect them.

Then a horrible thought came to Christiaan Eijkman. Suppose a germ did not cause beriberi at all!

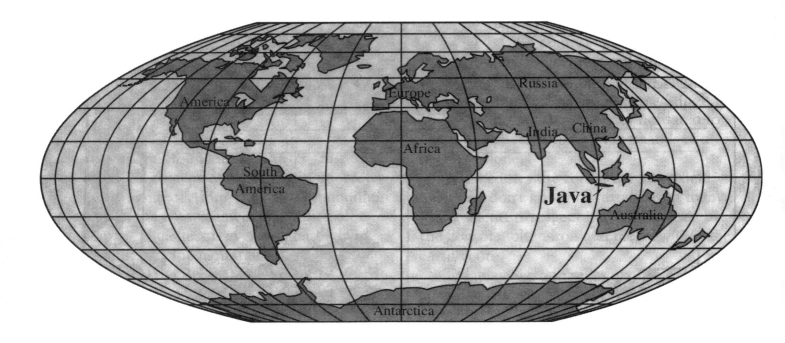

Because Robert Koch could not go, a former student, Christiaan Eijkman, was sent by the Dutch East India Company to Java to try to find the germ that causes beriberi and destroy it. The other doctors from the medical team could not find the germ and they left Java defeated. Eijkman refused to give up.

As he puzzled about this, the chickens did come down with beriberi. Their wings hung limp, and they stumbled around the chicken yard. All of them got the disease, even the ones that had not been a part of his experiment. He watched them closely. Days passed. The chickens got well.

Christiaan Eijkman became a detective. What had caused them to recover? Why had they come down with the beriberi in the first place? He looked for a clue to the mystery. He asked the cook, "What do you feed the chickens?"

"Brown rice," the cook explained. "Except last week I ran out of brown rice and used polished rice from the hospital storeroom. The hospital director made me stop. He says white rice is too expensive for chickens."

A simple experiment led Christiaan Eijkman to find the cause for beriberi. He separated the chickens into two groups. He fed brown rice to one group and polished rice to the other.

The "good" white rice caused beriberi — the "poor-quality" brown rice cured it! This explained why the natives seldom came down with the disease. The natives always ate brown rice. Settlers, on the other hand, ate rice that had been machine polished to remove the brown husks. Not only did white rice look better, but with the oily husks removed, it kept longer without spoiling.

"There must be something in the husks that the human body needs for good health," Eijkman concluded.

Christiaan Eijkman explained his discovery to the hospital director. Unfortunately the majority of doctors still considered beriberi to be a disease caused by germs. The hospital director dismissed Christiaan's discovery as nonsense.

"What!" the director cried. "You suspect the rice? Millions of people live on rice. It doesn't make them sick."

"They eat brown rice," Christiaan pointed out. "I suggest you buy brown rice for the patients."

The director grew stern. "You leave the choice of food to me! I'm afraid you've been wasting your time. Haven't you ever heard of Louis Pasteur? You'd serve your patients a good deal better if you'd start looking for the germ that causes beriberi." The director threw Eijkman's report aside.

Pasteur's success blinded doctors to the possibility that diseases might be caused in more than

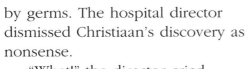

Eijkman found his answer by accident when chickens came down with the disease for no apparent reason. After a few days, the chickens recovered. Puzzled, he discovered that they had been fed white rice that week because they were out of brown rice. Eijkman then performed the experiment with a controlled group of chickens. He fed brown rice to one-half and white rice to the other. The white rice caused beriberi. The brown rice cured it.

one way. Six years passed. American doctors struggled to end an outbreak of beriberi in the Philippines. After all other means failed, they decided to feed their patients brown rice. Within two months that action wiped out the disease — except for four men who refused to eat the despised brown rice!

European settlers were eating white rice, rice that had been machine polished to remove the brown husks. Eijkman discovered the husks of the brown rice contained a vitamin that was needed for the prevention and cure of beriberi. Even after his discovery, many settlers died because they refused to eat the brown rice.

Christiaan Eijkman had shown that some diseases could be caused by the lack of certain chemicals that must be in the diet. Sometimes the amount of the chemical needed is so very slight that even a trace amount is enough to keep the body healthy.

Doctors eventually learned that the mysterious substance in the husks of rice is a vitamin called thiamine. Christiaan Eijkman's work no longer went unnoticed. In 1929 he was awarded the highest honor of the scientific world — the Nobel Prize in medicine.

Smallpox, rabies, and many other diseases are caused by bacteria and other microscopic living things that infect the body. But doctors cannot blame all diseases upon germs.

Dietary deficiency diseases like scurvy and beriberi are caused by the lack of vitamins. The word vitamin, coined in 1911, is from the Latin word vita meaning "life." Green vegetables, fruits, milk, grains, and meats all contain vitamins. They can be destroyed by long storage without refrigeration, by processing the food to keep it from spoiling, and by overcooking.

Unlike diseases caused by germs, dietary deficiency diseases are not contagious. No amount of contact with victims, their clothing, or body fluids will transfer the disease from a sick person to a healthy person.

Dietary diseases can also be caused by a lack of minerals. Both vitamins and minerals are chemicals. Vitamins are more complex substances usually produced by living things. Minerals are simple chemicals like salt, calcium, and iodine.

Goiter is an interesting example of a disease caused by the lack of a mineral, iodine. Iodine is a shiny, blue-black crystal. When solid iodine crystals are heated, they give off a rather beautiful violet vapor. The vapor, however, is poisonous.

The element iodine was discovered in 1811 by Bernard Courtois (pronounced koor-TWAH), a French chemist. Courtois collected seaweed washed ashore on beaches of Normandy and Brittany along the coast of France. He burned the seaweed to give ash. He washed the seaweed ash in hot sulfuric acid to purify it. On one occasion he mixed in too much acid. When he heated the mixture, it gave off a beautiful violet vapor. When Courtois cooled the violet vapor, it changed into dark, lustrous iodine crystals.

Iodine is a scarce element. It is found in sea water to some extent, but it is much less abundant on land. Several living things in the sea have the ability to concentrate iodine in their bodies. They become an important source for the element. Kelp, a large brown seaweed, is a

Seafood and iodized salt can supply the small amount of iodine needed by the thyroid gland to prevent simple goiter. Several diseases can be prevented simply by eating healthy food.

good source for iodine. Today iodine has many uses in medicine. Tincture of iodine is prepared from iodine. It is alcohol with iodine dissolved in it. Iodine in this form is painted on cuts to kill germs.

Iodine is also needed in the human diet to prevent goiter. This disease causes the thyroid gland at the front base of the neck to grow large and unattractive. The cure for goiter was discovered by Jean Boussingault (pronounced boo-sang-GOH), a French agricultural chemist.

The French chemist had read reports that certain salt deposits in South America prevented goiter. Upon checking a sample of the salt, he found that it contained iodine.

Jean Boussingault suggested that iodine might be a cure for goiter. At first, doctors did not take his suggestion seriously. Christiaan Eijkman's success over beriberi made them take a second look. Jean Boussingault was proven to be entirely correct.

We know now that the thyroid gland produces a chemical to regulate the speed at which the body uses food energy. The thyroid gland is located in the neck. Small amounts of iodine are essential in the diet to ensure proper functioning of the thyroid gland.

If the diet contains too little iodine, the thyroid gland may become enlarged. This condition is known as simple goiter. Doctors believe the body enlarges the thyroid gland to capture whatever iodine is available. The amount of iodine needed to prevent goiter is very slight indeed. The body of a healthy person contains about one two-hundredth of an ounce of iodine. Almost all of that is found in the thyroid gland.

For people who live by the sea, the slight amount of iodine in the water they drink or in the seafood they eat is enough to prevent goiter. For others, iodized table salt containing a small amount of iodide supplies the missing chemical. Iodized salt will reverse simple goiter or prevent its appearance. Iodine in larger amounts is toxic.

Good nutrition is no accident. Lack of vitamins and minerals in the diet can cause serious illnesses. This often results when unnecessary changes are made in the natural food God has provided.

When David of the Old Testament was a young man he spent much of his time in the outdoors. Most likely he learned to recognize the importance of fresh foods because he later wrote: "He [God] causeth the grass to grow for the cattle, and herb for the service of man: that he may bring forth food out of the earth" (Ps. 104:14).

DIAGNOSES

1. Christiaan Eijkman found that bacteria did not cause beriberi.

2. He found that brown rice was a cure for beriberi because of a vitamin (now known to be thiamine) in the husks.

3. Jean Boussingault found that a mineral called iodine could cure a goiter of the thyroid gland.

Answer T or F for true or false, or
Select A — D for the phrase that best completes the sentence.

A B   1. Beriberi means (A. *I cannot*; B. *scaly skin*).

T F   2. Robert Boyle recommended Christiaan Eijkman to the Dutch East India Company.

A B   3. Christian Eijkman went to (A. *Amsterdam, Holland*; B. *Java in the Pacific*) to treat beriberi.

T F   4. From the first, Christiaan Eijkman believed beriberi to be a dietary disease.

T F   5. Christiaan Eijkman was able to give chickens beriberi by injecting them with blood from human beriberi patients.

A B   6. Christiaan Eijkman concluded that beriberi could be prevented by (A. *eating brown rice*; B. *removing the husks of rice*).

T F   7. Christiaan Eijkman never received notice for his discovery of dietary diseases.

T F   8. Dietary diseases are especially contagious.

A B C D   9. Iodine in the diet prevents (A. *anthrax*; B. *beriberi*; C. *goiter*; D. *scurvy*).

T F   10. Lack of vitamins and minerals in the diet can cause serious illnesses.

Mysterious Rays

Zap! A spark jumped along the glass tube. William Crookes nodded. Yes, once the voltage built up, electricity cut through the air in the tube just like a tiny bolt of lightning.

What would happen when he drew most of the air out of the tube? Could electricity travel without air to conduct it? He didn't know, but he'd find out.

William Crookes was the son of a tailor — a wealthy tailor. He had inherited his father's huge fortune. With the money he built a private laboratory in his home in London, England.

The government of England often called upon William Crookes to solve problems in science. He made many practical inventions to help working people. For instance, he invented safety glasses to keep

SYMPTOMS

1. Could electricity travel without air to conduct it?

2. Could high voltage electricity be of any practical use?

3. Doctors were limited in diagnosing and treatment of patients by an inability to view inside the human body.

Can You Diagnose the Discoveries?

the blinding light of furnaces from hurting workers' eyes.

Unlike some scientists who grew old and set in their ways, William Crookes kept an active mind. He quickly took up new subjects. In the 1880s he became an expert in making glass tubes with nearly all of the air pumped out.

At the same time he became fascinated with high voltage electricity. An induction coil changes lower voltage to higher voltage. Crookes made one that generated thousands of volts.

He put the two studies together. Would high voltage electricity travel through a vacuum tube?

"Does it matter?" his wife asked. "Of what use is it?"

"Maybe no use," William Crookes said. "But I must know."

He hooked a positive electric terminal to one end of the tube and a negative electric terminal, known as a cathode, to the other end. He turned on the induction coil. The coil let him control the voltage: 1,000 volts, 5,000 volts, 10,000 volts.

Nothing seemed to be happening. He turned up the induction coil to its highest setting — 25,000 volts.

William Crookes, the son of a wealthy tailor, built a private laboratory in his home in London, England. There, after experimenting with vacuum glass tubes, he discovered cathode rays.

He experimented for hours. The sunlight streaming through his windows dimmed. Night fell. He stayed up, working late into the night. His wife and ten children went to bed. William Crookes went on experimenting. Gas lanterns cast flickering shadows on the walls.

His eyes adjusted to the dim light. Suddenly he peered closer at the tube. What was this? Instead of a sudden discharge, the tube glowed with a steady greenish light. He turned off the lights in his laboratory, plunging it into darkness. By the beautiful, pleasing glow, he saw the tube. It looked quite unlike anything he'd ever seen before.

The rays came from the end of the tube hooked to the negative (or cathode) terminal. William Crookes called them cathode rays. He wasn't satisfied with just giving them a name. He wondered, "What are they? Are the rays like light or like solid particles?"

He fussed around, trying to figure them out. Usually, the rays traveled in a straight line. But magnets bent their path, as did metal plates charged with electricity. Cathode rays couldn't be light rays.

Magnets and static electricity do not change the path of light. Instead, cathode rays had to be some kind of particles.

Several years passed before scientists discovered the exact nature of cathode rays. They are streams of very high-speed electrons. This was the first proof that atoms, the building blocks of matter, are themselves made of smaller building blocks, electrons.

In the United States, Thomas Edison learned how to make glass globes for his light bulbs from William Crookes' experiments. Other scientists filled Crookes' tube with neon gas. When they sent electricity through these neon lights, they glowed with carnival colors, bright and rather gaudy. They could bend neon tubes to spell words or trace out designs. They are used for advertising signs.

Crookes' tube became known as a cathode ray tube, abbreviated CRT. Today, cathode ray tubes are used for television and computer monitors.

Crookes' tube became known as a cathode ray tube, abbreviated CRT. Today, cathode ray tubes are used as television tubes and computer terminals.

William Crookes and his cathode rays may seem far removed from medicine. That turns out not to be the case. He had paved the way for one of the most dramatic and unexpected discoveries in the history of medicine.

On November 8, 1895, Wilhelm Roentgen (pronounced RUNT-gen) worked late into the afternoon. It was already dark. Roentgen experimented with a Crookes tube.

How far did cathode rays travel after they struck the walls of the glass tube? Some scientists believed the glass of the cathode tube stopped the rays in their tracks. Others believed they passed through the glass and traveled a short distance through the air.

Wilhelm Roentgen peered out at the world with intense eyes. He had a pale face that he hid behind a dark curling beard. He was a modest, precise man who did solid but unspectacular work. He was hardly known outside the University of Wurzburg in Bavaria where he taught physics.

He turned out the lights in the laboratory and turned on the Crookes tube. When he did, a glow from across the room caught his eye. It came from some crystals left over from an entirely different experiment. He turned off the cathode ray tube. The glow disappeared. He turned on the tube. The crystals glowed again.

Roentgen coated a piece of cardboard with the crystal. The cardboard glowed when rays from the Crookes tube struck it.

He experimented and found that the rays passed easily through thick pieces of wood and glass. He took a piece of paper coated with the crystal into the next room. It glowed even with the door closed. They passed through aluminum foil as easily as paper. But lead foil stopped them dead.

Could these be cathode rays? No, paper alone or a few inches of air stopped cathode rays. Cathode rays could not possibly reach the cardboard behind the closed door. Besides, magnets had no effect on the new rays, nor were their paths changed by static electricity.

Apparently the Crookes tube was generating rays other than the greenish glow scientists had observed before. Roentgen concluded, "I've discovered a second and new type of invisible ray."

One day he placed a sample in front of the cardboard screen. As he did, he saw a shadowy outline of his thumb on the screen. Wait! Inside the outline was a darker shadow of his bones. Incredible!

"Come, Emma!" he called to his wife. "Come here. You must see this."

She watched as he flexed his hand, seeing the joints move.

Wilhelm Roentgen taught physics at the University of Wurzburg in Bavaria. Here he did experiments with Crookes' tubes and made one of the ten most important medical discoveries of all time.

"We must take a picture of it," Roentgen decided. He wrapped photographic film in black paper and left it on the table under the Crookes' tube.

"Photographic film is not as sensitive to the invisible rays as the cardboard screen," he told her. He pressed her left hand on the film. "You'll have to hold still."

Patiently she kept her hand under the tube.

"Fifteen minutes," Roentgen said at last. "That's long enough."

He took the film to the darkroom. Finally he came out. Triumphantly he held the still wet glass plate. "It worked," he said. "It shows the bones of your hand in full detail. The image is negative — your bones show as white, and the skin is dark."

"What's the white circle?" Emma asked.

"Your wedding ring," Roentgen explained. "The gold entirely stops the invisible rays."

"The rays need a name," his wife suggested.

Thoughtfully, Roentgen agreed.

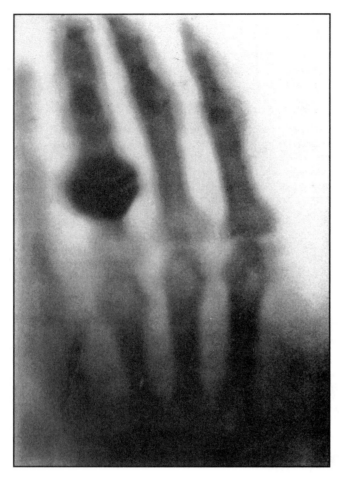

An x-ray of Roentgen's wife's hand showing the bones in her hand and also her gold wedding ring. Never before had doctors been able to see through human skin and view the bones beneath.

"Mathematicians use (x) to stand for the unknown. I'll call them x-rays."

"You must tell others about this," Emma said.

"Not yet," Roentgen said. "The discovery seems so mysterious it lies outside what scientists know. Without more facts to back me up, I'll not be believed. 'Invisible rays that see through human flesh? Impossible!' they'll say."

Emma warned, "If you wait too long someone else will stumble upon the discovery."

She's right, Roentgen thought to himself. He was torn between his need to experiment and the desire to tell others about the rays. He delayed the announcement as long as he dared. For seven weeks he frantically experimented.

Finally, on December 22, 1895, he announced the discovery. He also asked to speak before the next meeting of the Physical Medicine Society of Wurzburg, Germany.

At a meeting on January 23, 1896, Roentgen stood before the professors, scientists, and doctors. He delivered a lecture titled "On the discovery of a new kind of ray." They greeted the news with polite, but stony silence. He could see the doubtful looks on their faces. How could he get beyond their unbelief?

He offered to take an x-ray on the spot. "I have brought my equipment with me," he told them. "I need a volunteer from the audience."

A well-known and elderly doctor, Albrecht von Koffiker, stood up. "I will try."

"It will take some time," Roentgen warned the 80-year-old man.

The stern old doctor scowled at Roentgen, irritated at the suggestion he might be too old to hold his hand motionless long enough. Roentgen set up the apparatus and turned it on.

After 15 minutes he removed the photograph and had it developed. It had worked to perfection. Kolliker's hand showed clearly. The bones and joints between them could be traced out. The meeting broke up in wild applause.

Some scientists walked forward to shake Roentgen's hand. Others jumped up and ran for the exits. They raced to their laboratories to try it for themselves.

Most research laboratories already had Crookes' tubes. Moments after getting back to their laboratories, scientists could repeat Roentgen's experiments. X-rays took the scientific world by storm. Within a year, more than a thousand research papers had been written on the subject.

Some people tried to name the rays Roentgen rays in his honor. But people who don't speak German found the name "Roentgen" difficult to pronounce. Besides, the name x-rays caught the public fancy, so Roentgen's original name for his discovery is the one used today.

In 1912 the nature of x-rays was found. Cathode rays are made of streams of fast-moving electrons. When the electrons strike the target at the other end of the cathode ray tube, they stop suddenly. The sudden stop changes their energy into high-power light rays. X-rays, then, are like ultraviolet light, but much more powerful and more penetrating.

Doctors put x-rays to practical use. Only four days after the news of Roentgen's discovery reached America, doctors used x-rays to locate a bullet in a patient's leg. X-rays gave doctors a new tool of astonishing power. Was a bullet near the heart? Take an x-ray. A child had swallowed a safety pin — was it open or closed? X-rays answered the question. Had the factory worker broken his leg, or was it merely sprained? X-rays showed the finest hairline fracture. Dentists took x-rays to find decayed spots on teeth.

Doctors wanted to see more. They wanted to look at the stomach, intestines, and blood vessels. X-rays normally don't show skin, flesh, and blood. These soft body parts are made of lightweight atoms: hydrogen, carbon, nitrogen, and oxygen. On the other hand, bones and teeth show up because the body's skeleton and teeth are of heavier atoms: calcium and phosphorus.

How could doctors make soft tissues visible in x-rays?

An American, Walter Cannon, solved the problem. He mixed a "milk shake" of barium sulfate for his patients. Barium is an element of high atomic weight. Once it coats the stomach and intestines, they become visible in x-rays.

Roentgen refused to patent his invention. "It's too important to medicine," he said. In 1903, the Nobel Prize committee awarded him the first Nobel Prize in physics for his discovery. It was the only money he ever received for his invention.

Roentgen's x-rays created an immense

Below is a modern day MRI (Magnetic Resonance Imaging) scan that shows a top and side view of a human head. MRI and other medical technologies scan the body from any angle or direction without surgery. The image reveals a particular layer as a still picture. Or, the doctor can see an organ in action, such as the beating of the heart, as a series of moving images.

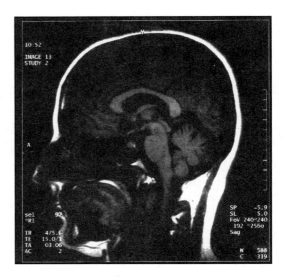

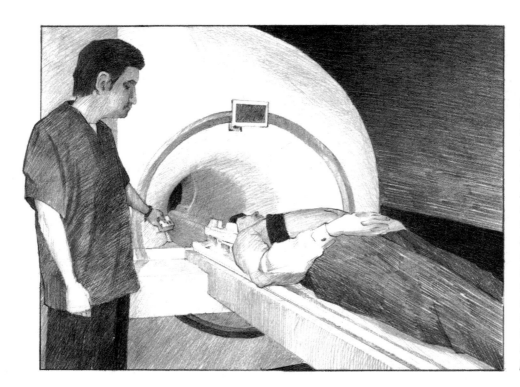

This doctor is guiding a patient into an MRI Scanner at Northwest Arkansas Medical Imaging, Inc. in Fayetteville, Arkansas. An MRI scan gives doctors the knowledge they need without invasive surgery. Because the MRI works using large magnets and computers instead of radiation, it is much safer for the patient.

sensation, not only in scientific circles, but among the general public, too. Amusement parks put x-ray machines in fun houses and coated screens with zinc sulfide. Visitors could stand before the screen and see their own skeletons.

Shoe stores used the machines, too. Customers could check whether new shoes cramped their toes.

All in all, people took entirely too many x-rays. The first person to call attention to the dangers of x-rays was Thomas Edison. The new rays poisoned one of his assistants. The man's hair fell out and his scalp became covered with sores.

Edison and other scientists warned against needless use of x-rays. Sadly, their calls for caution went unheeded for many years. Some people suffered terrible radiation burns from overexposure to x-rays. We know now that x-rays can damage living cells. Exposure must be for short periods of time.

On the other hand, cancer cells are more easily killed by x-rays than healthy tissue. Cancer can sometimes be controlled by treating the cells with x-rays.

The discovery of x-rays is one of the ten most important discoveries in medicine, primarily for the ability of x-rays to allow doctors to see the condition of organs within the human body.

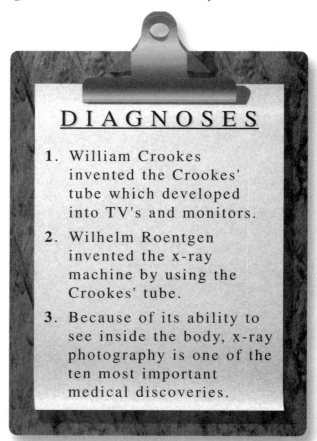

DIAGNOSES

1. William Crookes invented the Crookes' tube which developed into TV's and monitors.

2. Wilhelm Roentgen invented the x-ray machine by using the Crookes' tube.

3. Because of its ability to see inside the body, x-ray photography is one of the ten most important medical discoveries.

> *Answer T or F for true or false, or*
> *Select A — D for the phrase that best completes the sentence.*

T F 1. William Crookes was the son of a wealthy tailor.

T F 2. As he grew older, William Crookes became set in his ways.

A B C 3. Crookes saw the glow from the tube because he (A. *awoke early in the morning*; B. *stayed up after dark*; C. *used special glasses that he invented*).

T F 4. Magnets and static electricity change the path of light.

A B C D 5. Cathode rays are actually streams of (A. *helium atoms*; B. *high-speed electrons*; C. *infrared light*; D. *high-power light rays*).

A B A 6. Crookes' tube filled with neon gas is used to make (A. *advertising signs*; B. *x-rays*).

A B C D 7. X-rays are actually streams of (A. *helium atoms*; B. *high-speed electrons*; C. *infrared light*; D. *high-power light rays*).

A B 8. Roentgen called his discovery x-rays because they were (A. *unknown*; B. *came from a Xenon tube*).

T F 9. Most laboratories had the equipment to generate x-rays.

A B C D 10. X-rays can be used to (A. *find bullets in a body*; B. *tell if a leg is broken*; C. *find decayed spots on teeth*; D. *all three*).

T F 11. Wilhelm Roentgen patented his invention.

T F 12. Wilhelm Roentgen received the first Nobel Prize in physics for his discovery.

> *Select the matching letter from the list below.*

13. _____ was the first to experiment with high-voltage electrical discharge in a vacuum tube.

14. _____ discovered x-rays.

15. _____ invented a barium sulfate milk shake to show soft body parts by x-rays.

16. _____ warned about the dangers of x-rays.

| A. *Walter Cannon* |
| B. *William Crookes* |
| C. *Thomas Edison* |
| D. *Wilhelm Roentgen* |

Useful Radiation

Roentgen's discovery of x-rays excited all of science. Not since the time of Galileo had anything shaken the scientific world so thoroughly. Many scientists had grown smug and self-satisfied, thinking they had all the answers. Roentgen's unexpected discovery left these scientists completely astounded. Very quickly, experiments uncovered other wonderful findings. The year 1895 marked the first year of a decade that became known as the second scientific revolution.

Henri Becquerel, a Frenchman, saw x-ray photographs for the first time on January 20, 1896. Wilhelm Roentgen had sent them to the French Academy of Sciences. Thoughtfully, Becquerel examined the photographs.

Until then Henri Becquerel

SYMPTOMS

1. Some people were overusing x-ray machines and were suffering from radiation burns.

2. Were there other materials that would improve the x-ray?

3. Could x-rays be used to help fight disease?

Can You Diagnose the Discoveries?

had studied fluorescent crystals. These crystals glow when struck by ultraviolet light. Special lamps are needed to give off ultraviolet light, or sunlight itself can be used.

"I don't want to merely repeat Roentgen's work," Henri Becquerel told his friend Pierre Curie. "I'll strike out in a new direction."

"Maybe ultraviolet light will cause your fluorescent crystals to emit x-rays, too," Pierre Curie suggested.

Henri Becquerel decided to try an unusual experiment. "I'll wrap a piece of photographic film in thick paper so sunlight can't get through. Then I'll put a fluorescent crystal on it and leave them in bright sunlight. If the crystal does change ultraviolet light to x-rays, they will go through the paper and fog the film."

He set the photographic plate with the crystal upon it out in the bright sunlight for a few hours. When he developed the film it was only slightly fogged. "It needs more time in the sunlight," he decided.

He wrapped a fresh piece of film and set it outside. Clouds rolled in right away and covered the sky. Henri Becquerel put aside the fresh film in a desk drawer.

When Henri Becquerel, a Frenchman, accidentally had some X-ray film exposed by a mysterious substance, he knew that he was onto a major discovery. He then began his search for useful radiation.

Days passed. The bad weather showed no signs of going away. Growing restless, he developed the film anyway. He expected the film to be clear. After all, the crystal had been exposed to sunlight for only a few minutes. To his amazement, the film was nearly black. It had darkened as though exposed to bright light.

"What can be the reason for this?" he wondered. Henri Becquerel wrapped another piece of film and left it in the desk drawer. After waiting as long as he could bear, he developed the film.

Becquerel explained to Pierre Curie what must have happened. "I keep several different samples of crystals and ores in my desk. One of them must have given off invisible rays, perhaps even x-rays," he concluded. "They penetrated the paper and exposed the film."

"But which one?" Pierre asked.

By a series of experiments Henri Becquerel eliminated one sample after another. Finally, he found the source. It was pitchblende, an ore of uranium.

A German chemist named Martin Klaproth discovered uranium more than a hundred years earlier. He could find no

Pierre and Marie Curie worked together as a husband and wife team on all their scientific experiments. Marie coined the term "radioactivity" to describe the properties of the substances that they worked so hard to discover.

particular use for the metal. Klaproth feared his discovery would soon be forgotten. The planet Uranus had been discovered a few years earlier. So Klaproth named the metal after the planet Uranus in an effort to keep it before the public eye.

Uranium does give off invisible rays. It does so all on its own. Ultraviolet light isn't needed. Uranium atoms undergo radioactive decay. All of a sudden a uranium atom will break apart. It throws out powerful x-rays and other particles.

Although Klaproth discovered uranium in 1792, its radioactive nature had gone unnoticed for a hundred years. After Henri Becquerel's discovery in 1896, uranium became famous. It is still the most common radioactive element.

During all of this Henri Becquerel talked at length about his project with Pierre Curie and Pierre's new bride, Marie. The Curies offered helpful suggestions to Henri. In fact, Marie coined the name "radioactivity" for what he observed.

Henri Becquerel said, "I've proven that radiation from uranium is like x-rays, but even more powerful."

"Are other elements radioactive?" Pierre wondered.

Henri Becquerel shrugged. "I've not looked into that idea. My uranium studies take all of my time." He suggested that the Curies start the hunt for other radioactive substances.

They readily agreed. Marie began the search for radioactive elements in 1896. Excited, she found pitchblende to be radioactive, even with uranium removed. Marie said, "It is even more strongly radioactive than uranium itself. Pitchblende must contain more than one radioactive element."

In 1898 the Curies isolated a new element from pitchblende. It turned out to be radioactive. They named it polonium after Poland, Marie's native land.

Even the presence of uranium and polonium could not account for all the radioactivity that came from pitchblende. Another element remained. Although they did not actually see the element causing the radiation, they gave it a name: radium. Its name comes from the Latin word radius meaning "ray."

Finally, in 1902 the husband and wife team collected enough radium to fill a tiny glass tube. In all they went through

By working with Becquerel, Pierre and Marie Curie were able to discover radium, which is 100 million times more radioactive than an equal amount of pure uranium. The glow of their new discovery lights their faces.

six tons of pitchblende to extract about 1/300 of an ounce of pure radium.

It turns out that radium is 100 million times more radioactive than an equal amount of pure uranium. For a few years clockmakers used radium in numbers and hands on clock faces. The clocks could be seen at night. Watchmakers stopped the practice when they discovered the dangers of radiation poisoning.

Rays given off by radium can destroy human tissue. Henri Becquerel learned this when he carried a sample of radium with him. He suffered a bad burn because of it.

Radioactive material can destroy human tissue. However, when carefully controlled, radium can destroy cancer growths in the human body. Some cancer cells are more sensitive to radioactive rays than normal cells. When exposed to rays from radium, cancer cells are destroyed but healthy cells survive. This process immediately took its place as another powerful tool in the treatment of disease. The process is known as radiotherapy.

When doctors realized that radium could fight cancer, it became one of the most sought-after materials in the world. Paris opened a "radium hospital."

Elements not normally radioactive can be made so by exposing them to radioactivity. The body can't tell the difference between a regular element and the same one after it has been made radioactive. Certain organs of the body absorb some chemical elements more than they absorb others. Bones contain a larger proportion of calcium than the rest of the body. The thyroid gland contains an abundance of iodine.

Radioactive iodine fights thyroid cancer. It is mixed with a special salt. The patient eats the salt, and the radioactive iodine is carried to the diseased thyroid gland in the patient's neck. There the iodine builds up, causing the tumor to wither and die.

Just as iodine is picked up by one gland of the body, so other parts of the

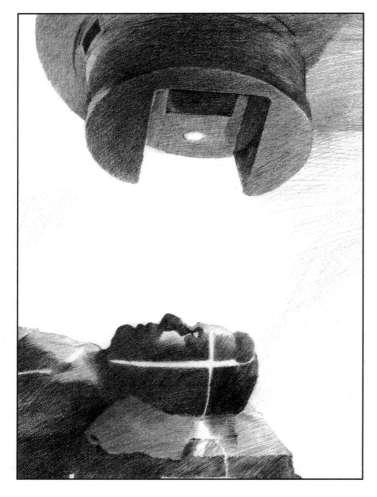

This patient is undergoing modern radiation therapy to destroy the cancer in his body. When controlled, the radiation can kill the dangerous cancer cells and let the healthy tissue survive. God created the forces of nature for the benefit of mankind. We must discover the proper ways to use them.

body collect other chemicals. Radioactive gold settles in the liver. Phosphorus ends up in the bones. Chromium is taken up by the red blood cells. By making these elements radioactive and finding harmless ways of giving them to patients, cancer in various parts of the body can be treated.

In addition to radiotherapy, radioactive elements are used as tracers. The motion of trace amounts of radioactive elements can be followed throughout the body. Only very minute amounts of radioactive elements are needed, far less than would cause injury.

For example, minerals in plant food are made radioactive. By means of a Geiger counter, a scientist can follow the carbon and see how the plant uses it. What can be done with plants can be done with the human body, too.

Suppose a medical researcher wants to learn how a new drug works. He can use a radioactive tracer, carbon perhaps, in the manufacture of the drug. Doctors watch the dose of the radioactive drug as it goes through the body. They learn how much is in the blood at various times, how fast it passes out of the body, and where some of it collects in the body.

Isn't it interesting to observe the dual nature of radiation? Used carelessly it causes pain and injury. Used cautiously it becomes a powerful tool for fighting disease. God created the forces of nature for the benefit of mankind. We must discover the proper ways to use them.

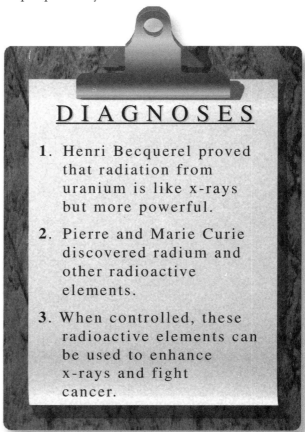

DIAGNOSES

1. Henri Becquerel proved that radiation from uranium is like x-rays but more powerful.

2. Pierre and Marie Curie discovered radium and other radioactive elements.

3. When controlled, these radioactive elements can be used to enhance x-rays and fight cancer.

> *Answer T or F for true or false, or*
> *Select A — D for the phrase that best completes the sentence.*

A B   1. The one who discovered x-rays was (A. *Henri Becquerel*; B. *Wilhelm Roentgen*).

T F   2. The discovery of x-rays had little effect upon the scientific world.

A B   3. The year 1895 marked the first year of the (A. *industrial revolution*; B. *second scientific revolution*).

A B   4. The one who discovered that pitchblende is radioactive was (A. *Pierre Curie*; B. *Henri Becquerel*).

A B   5. Becquerel's film was exposed by (A. *bright sunlight*; B. *an ore in his desk*).

A B C D   6. Pitchblende is an ore of (A. *calcium*; B. *iodine*; C. *phosphorus*; D. *uranium*).

T F   7. Uranium was named after the planet Uranus.

A B   8. The one who coined the name radioactivity was (A. *Thomas Edison*; B. *Marie Curie*).

A B C   9. The most radioactive element that the Curies found was (A. *polonium*; B. *radium*; C. *uranium*).

T F   10. Radioactivity can kill cancer cells but is harmless to human tissue.

T F   11. A tracer is a radioactive element used to coat bullets.

Wonder Drugs

The first person to glimpse bacteria was Antoni van Leeuwenhoek in 1683. Later, several types of bacteria were identified. Staphylococci bacteria cause staph infections. Streptococci bacteria causes strep throat. Pneumococci bacteria causes pneumonia.

During the next two centuries, Joseph Lister fought infection by keeping bacteria out of the body. Edward Jenner, Louis Pasteur, and Robert Koch developed vaccinations to help the body's own defenses against invading bacteria. The body uses its white blood cells to fight invading bacteria. Usually the white blood cells conquer the bacteria. Sometimes, however, the bacteria are too strong. They multiply in the body and overwhelm the white blood cells. As late as the 1930s

SYMPTOMS

1. Doctors still had no drugs to fight many common diseases.

2. Doctors needed something that would kill bacteria without harming human tissue.

3. Some bacteria were overwhelming the body's natural defenses.

Can You Diagnose the Discoveries?

doctors still had no drug to fight many of the most common and most dangerous diseases. Antiseptics, applied externally, were still the most common way to deal with bacteria.

The problem doctors faced is to kill the bacteria without harming human tissue. It's easy to find chemicals that kill germs, but they usually kill the patient, too. In fact, most antiseptics are better at killing the helpful white blood cells than at killing bacteria. A useful drug is one that destroys bacteria without having bad side effects upon the patient.

This is the way things were until a German chemical company decided to plow some of its profits into medical research.

In the early 1900s, the German chemical industry led the world in the production of artificial dyes. The most successful of these firms was I.G. Farben. The company made a variety of synthetic chemicals. The company built a well-equipped laboratory to test its chemicals for their medical properties. The company leaders thought that one or

more of their many chemicals might combat disease.

One of the doctors employed in the chemical laboratory was Gerhard Domagk. Gerhard Domagk (pronounced DOH-mahkh) had been born in the little town of Lagow, Germany, in 1895. He showed a great interest in medicine and read all the medical books he could find. He intended to become a doctor.

Just as he turned 18 years old and enrolled in medical school, World War I began. Medical school had to wait.

Gerhard Domagk's commanding officers made him a battlefield medic. Although self-taught, he knew far more than the average doctor. By the end of the war he'd become an accomplished physician. After the war he made it official by earning a medical degree.

In 1927, the I.G. Farben company had asked Dr. Domagk to join their staff. At first he hesitated. What could a doctor do in a chemical factory? He learned he would still be saving lives. He would

Gerhard Domagk was born in Lagow, Germany, in 1895. He served as a medic in World War I, then after the war he earned his medical degree. He worked for I.G. Farben company to study chemicals that combat disease.

This petri dish contains a bacterial culture which is being grown by scientists for study. A single culture can contain hundreds of thousands of the bacteria. The Streptococci bacteria that cause strep throat are shown magnified several hundred times the actual size.

study new dyes, not for the use of coloring fabrics, but for possible uses in medicine.

Chemists at the German dye company made a bright red compound which they patented under the name Prontosil. They made the dye from coal tar, a black, sticky substance.

In 1932 Domagk infected mice with a deadly strain of staph bacteria. Then he injected Prontosil. To his great pleasure, the dye completely reversed the infection. Domagk put the dye to a very personal use. His own daughter's life was threatened by a serious infection. She'd pricked herself with a needle. Nothing the doctors tried helped. Her condition became more desperate as the bacteria causing the infection multiplied.

Domagk administered a massive injection of Prontosil to his daughter. Her condition improved dramatically. With that success behind him, Domagk published a report of the drug's extraordinary powers in 1932.

Only a part of the complex chemical of Prontosil actually destroyed bacteria. Chemists identified the active agent as sulfanilamide. It could be made much more quickly and easily than the dye itself. Sulfanilamide was the forerunner of a whole family of antiseptic sulfa drugs, which came from the chemical laboratory.

Sulfa drugs have not been found in nature. They are strictly synthetic, made in the chemical laboratory.

In the United States, Dr. Perrin H. Long at Johns Hopkins University became interested in the drug. In the summer of 1936 he attended a scientific meeting in London. There he learned of Prontosil and its role in fighting infection. Dr. Long immediately ordered samples of sulfa to experiment with once he returned to the United States.

His experiments confirmed the wonderful properties of sulfa. Not only did it combat deadly infections, but it seldom brought on harmful side effects.

In November of 1936 the White House called Johns Hopkins University Hospital. Franklin Roosevelt Jr., the 22-year-old son of the president, had a very serious infection of the throat.

"His physician considers his condition serious," Mrs. Roosevelt explained.

"He's dying. Will the sulfa drug help?"

Dr. Long agreed to treat the president's son. He rushed to the bedside of the young man and began treatment with sulfa. The younger Roosevelt showed immediate improvement. He soon was out of danger. The successful treatment made headlines across the country and around the world.

Seldom had a new discovery become

Sulfa was a wonderful discovery because it killed one-celled bacteria but did not hurt the cells of human tissue. This picture shows a soldier being treated with an application of sulfa. The drug saved many lives. During the time period of World War II, more soldiers were dying from infections and diseases than from bombs and bullets.

SULFA POWDER

so well-known so quickly. Newspapers called sulfa a "wonder drug." The wonder is that it killed one-celled bacteria but did not hurt the cells of human tissue. In fact, sulfa drugs can be given in massive amounts without being toxic. During the fighting of World War II, medics freely sprinkled the drug in open wounds before they tied on bandages.

The Nobel Prize committee saw the importance of Domagk's discovery. In 1939 they awarded the Nobel Prize in medicine to him. This was only seven years after his announcement, which is very fast action indeed for the Nobel committee. At first, Dr. Domagk wrote a letter accepting the prize. The committee was puzzled by a second letter that he wrote a few weeks later. In the second letter he coldly turned down the award.

Later, the truth came out. In that same year, the Nobel committee awarded the Peace Prize to another German, Karl von Ossietzky. This man opposed Hitler and had been thrown into a Nazi concentration camp for his trouble. Hitler kept Karl von Ossietzky from accepting the Peace Prize.

In anger, Hitler also ordered Dr. Domagk to turn down his Nobel award in medicine. Gerhard Domagk refused. The Gestapo, the Nazi secret police, arrested him and jailed him for a week. They dictated the second letter in which he refused the Nobel Prize.

A gold medal and large cash award accompanied the prize. Dr. Domagk never received the money, which was turned back to the Nobel committee. In 1947, after World War II and the death of Hitler, Dr. Domagk visited Stockholm. He delivered his lecture and received his gold medal.

How does sulfa kill bacteria? Usually it is difficult to learn exactly how a drug works. In the case of sulfa, however, the reason is easily understood. The action is due to a case of mistaken identity. Some disease bacteria need a certain acid to grow and multiply. Bacteria take this acid from human blood.

The acid and sulfa are very much alike. Bacteria can't tell the two compounds apart. Instead of taking the acid from the blood, they accept sulfa and make it part of their body. But without the acid, the bacteria die. The infection clears up.

Sulfa does not fool all types of bacteria, so it is not a universal cure-all. Sulfa did enjoy a time of immense importance until shortly after World War II. Then even better antibiotics replaced it. Sulfa was the first wonder drug.

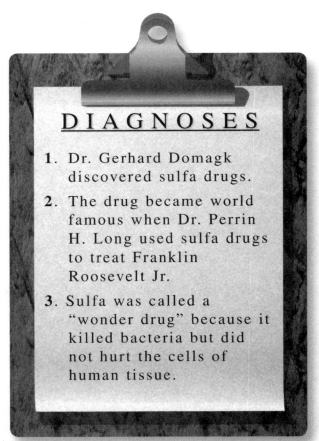

DIAGNOSES

1. Dr. Gerhard Domagk discovered sulfa drugs.

2. The drug became world famous when Dr. Perrin H. Long used sulfa drugs to treat Franklin Roosevelt Jr.

3. Sulfa was called a "wonder drug" because it killed bacteria but did not hurt the cells of human tissue.

Answer T or F for true or false, or
Select A or B for the phrase that best completes the sentence.

T F   1. It is easy to find chemicals that kill germs.

A B   2. Gerhard Domagk studied uses of dyes in (A. coloring fabrics; B. medicine).

T F   3. Sulfa drugs come from a tree found in South America.

A B   4. The treatment of President Franklin Roosevelt's son was (A. done in secret; B. made newspaper headlines).

T F   5. Sulfa is a wonder drug because it kills one-celled bacteria but not human tissue.

T F   6. Sulfa drugs must be given in strictly measured doses.

A B   7. Dr. Domagk refused the Nobel Prize because (A. Hitler ordered him to turn it down; B. Americans received partial credit for his discovery).

T F   8. Sulfa is a universal cure-all for infection.

Select the matching letter from the list below.

9. _____ was the first person to glimpse bacteria.
10. _____ fought infection by keeping bacteria out of the body.
11. _____ developed vaccination.
12. _____ served as a medic during World War I.
13. _____ brought news of sulfa drugs to America.

A. Gerhard Domagk
B. Edward Jenner
C. Antoni van Leeuwenhoek
D. Joseph Lister
E. Perrin H. Long

Mold Battles Bacteria

Sulfa enjoyed a time of immense popularity. But even before it came into general use, penicillin, the most important of all antibiotics, had already been discovered.

Alexander Fleming, a Scottish physician, served in the Royal Army Medical Corps during World War I. After the war he attended St. Mary's Medical School in London and graduated with honors. He chose to stay on at St. Mary's Medical School as a teacher rather than seeking a job elsewhere.

St. Mary's was an old-fashioned school. Alexander Fleming's equipment at St. Mary's was rather simple and limited. He outfitted his laboratory in a roughly furnished basement room. An open window provided ventilation. Dust and leaves drifted in with the fresh air. His conference room

S Y M P T O M S

1. Sulfa did not work on all types of bacteria.

2. More research was needed to find other germ fighting chemicals.

3. Some antibiotics were so hard to make that they were too expensive to be practical.

Can You Diagnose the Discoveries?

was a nearby park bench under a huge elm tree. Despite the primitive conditions, Dr. Fleming did what he could.

During one experiment, he grew some deadly little staph bacteria. He wanted to learn more about them for a book he was writing. Staph bacteria cause boils and other infections. Dr. Fleming grew the bacteria on the surface of a jelly-like food in shallow petri dishes.

For several days, the colonies of staph had been growing on the jelly-like food.

One day as Dr. Fleming examined a dish he saw that it had become moldy. A mold spore had fallen through the basement window and into the petri dish.

Suddenly, he peered closer. He saw a circle of clear liquid around the deadly staph bacteria. The dark green mold had dissolved it. What had been a well-grown staph colony was now a faint shadow of its former self.

Alexander Fleming identified the foreign mold as penicillium, a type of bread mold. Like all molds, penicillium is a tiny living organism, which belongs to the fungi group. When Alexander Fleming worked with pencillium, it was clasified as a plant, although like mushrooms and mildew it contained no chlorophyll. Penicillium develops from spores. A spore falls upon food and begins growing by putting out hair-like roots.

Alexander Fleming, a Scottish physician, discovered penicillin. Fleming served in the Royal Army Medical Corps during World War I. He then attended St. Mary's in London and graduated with honors. In a basement lab of this institute Fleming made his discovery of penicillin.

Alexander Fleming correctly guessed that penicillium mold releases a chemical that kills germs. He named the chemical penicillin.

Although a chance discovery, Dr. Fleming instantly grasped its significance. Suppose he'd worked in a clean and spotless laboratory. Suppose a chance breeze through the basement window had not carried the mold spore? Suppose Fleming himself had cleaned the dish and put it away without investigating? Then one of the most powerful drugs known would have gone undetected.

Of course, the new chemical might also damage human cells. All the germ killers then in common use were as dangerous to the host as they were to bacteria. To be useful, a substance should destroy bacteria without being toxic to the patient.

Dr. Fleming transplanted a bit of the

Penicillin was originally found in a type of mold (left). It took so long for Fleming to grow a culture that it was too expensive for practical use. It can now be mass produced and can be administered in many ways: pills, injections, or liquid.

mold into new petri dishes. Slowly his petri dish garden yielded enough mold for him to experiment further. He injected mice with it. The mice survived unharmed. Apparently, the mold produced a chemical that killed bacteria but not the cells of larger organisms. Here was something special.

Growing the mold, extracting the penicillin, and concentrating it took too much time. Dr. Fleming never developed enough to tackle real diseases. Each precious sample could only be used for trial cases. To make it in quantity, he needed assistants trained in chemistry and a better laboratory.

Alexander Fleming was a physician, not a chemist. In May 1929 he reported the discovery and invited any interested chemist to pursue the matter. The report aroused little interest.

For almost ten years his paper on penicillin lay forgotten on the library shelves. Then sulfa came on the scene, and captured world attention when it saved the life of Franklin Roosevelt Jr., son of the American president.

Until the success of sulfa, few doctors believed chemicals taken into the body could have medicinal value against bacteria. They still believed vaccination was the way to prevent infectious diseases.

Sulfa proved that chemicals could make dramatic breakthroughs in fighting disease. If one chemical such as sulfa could destroy bacteria, then maybe others could, too.

When World War II began in 1939 the search for infection-preventing chemicals became more urgent. More people died from disease and infection than from bullets and bombs. Several big firms in England followed the lead of I.G. Farben in Germany. They offered research grants for doctors to look for disease killers. Dr. Howard Walter Florey, an Australian physician, received a large sum of money for his investigation. He had two advantages preparing him for a future success. He was a researcher at the well-equipped Oxford University laboratory, and he had a brilliant assistant, Ernst Chain.

Florey and Chain did their homework. They read hundreds of back issues of medical journals. They came up with three articles about the work already done in the field. One of the three articles was Fleming's original paper. Florey and Chain traveled to St. Mary's to talk personally with Fleming.

Howard Walter Florey, an Australian physician (left), and his assistant, Ernst Chain (right), working in a lab at Oxford University isolated penicillin, the actual chemical involved. They found the pure form was even more powerful than Fleming had ever dreamed. In 1945, Alexander Fleming, Walter Florey, and Ernst Chain shared the Nobel Prize in medicine for their discovery.

Dr. Fleming had not given up completely on penicillin. He still kept a precious sample of the original mold alive. For ten years he'd grown it, transplanted it from one petri dish to another, and kept it at the right temperature. Dr. Fleming gave Florey and Chain a sample to take back to Oxford with them.

The Oxford scientists succeeded in isolating penicillin, the actual chemical involved. They found that penicillin in the pure form was even more powerful than Fleming had dreamed. It took two years of hard work before they grew enough penicillin to treat a human patient.

In a nearby hospital, the doctors were trying to save the life of a policeman. The Oxford "bobby" had nicked himself while shaving. Infection set in. His temperature soared. Sulfa drugs proved to be useless. The policeman's doctors did not believe he would live another day. They heard of Florey's work and asked him to treat their patient.

Florey diluted the drug so he could stretch it over several doses. After the first injection, the policeman's temperature dropped and his breathing became easier.

His face, which had been red and puffed, began to look normal.

The next day the temperature went up again. Florey gave the man another shot of penicillin. Again, the policeman improved. By the fourth day, the doctors could see that the patient would recover. Then, horrified, they learned that Florey had run out of penicillin. It would take him weeks to make more. The doctors watched helplessly as the patient's temperature rose. Finally, he died.

Penicillin was horribly expensive. For that single patient it had cost a thousand dollars a day. "It's not practical," most doctors decided. "It takes too long to make enough penicillin to do a patient any good."

Despite the setback, Florey knew penicillin was even more important than sulfa. It wreaked havoc on bacteria that sulfa couldn't touch. Penicillin had fewer dangerous side effects. A thousandfold overdose could be given before it became toxic.

"We simply must reduce the cost, " Florey said.

Chain agreed. "Penicillin needs to be

manufactured by the ton, not by the ounce."

Because the bombing of World War II made England a poor site for chemical studies, the English scientists asked doctors in the United States for help. In the summer of 1941 Ernst Chain flew to America. He carried with him a vial of penicillin mold. It was a remote descendent of the original speck that had settled in Dr. Fleming's petri dish 12 years earlier.

American scientists quickly discovered ways to grow penicillium in quantity. Mold would grow within a jelly-like food, as well as on its surface. They built huge vats with paddles to stir the mixture. The mold grew all through it. American mass production turned out penicillin as easily as it turned out cars.

In January 1943 they purified only two ounces. By September, two pounds. By year's end, a thousand pounds.

Penicillin became the doctors' best weapon for fighting infections. It fought bacteria that caused meningitis, pneumonia, strep throat, and bone and blood infections. Although it does not kill the bacteria, it apparently prevents them from forming a protective cell wall. It weakens the germs so the body's own defenses can finish them off.

For Dr. Fleming the years of discouragement of trying to interest people in penicillin ended. Recognition came to him. He was knighted — Sir Alexander Fleming.

In 1945, Alexander Fleming, Walter Florey, and Ernst Chain shared the Nobel Prize in medicine for their discovery.

Doctors still battled infections by bacteria that resisted the action of penicillin. Maybe other molds would fight these diseases. This idea set off a mold hunt that is still going on. The search has discovered streptomycin and other antibiotics like penicillin.

Although penicillin can be made from scratch in the laboratory, the process is much too expensive. Molds do it better. However, chemists have learned to stop molds in mid-step, so to speak. They separate a partially completed penicillin molecule. To this core, they tack on other chemicals. These tailor-made antibiotics are sometimes better than penicillin itself.

For a time in the early 1950s doctors hoped diseases could be eliminated one by one by developing the right wonder drugs. This turned out not to be the case. Micro-organisms develop a resistance to the drugs used against them. Doctors must constantly search for new chemicals to combat new strains of disease germs.

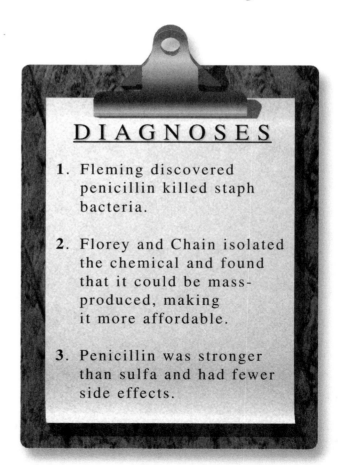

DIAGNOSES

1. Fleming discovered penicillin killed staph bacteria.

2. Florey and Chain isolated the chemical and found that it could be mass-produced, making it more affordable.

3. Penicillin was stronger than sulfa and had fewer side effects.

Answer T or F for true or false, or
Select A or B for the phrase that best completes the sentence.

A B   1. At St. Mary's, Dr. Fleming's conference room was (A. a classroom; B. a park bench).

A B   2. The staph bacteria had been dissolved by a mold spore that (A. Dr. Fleming introduced into the petri dish; B. came in through an open window).

T F   3. Penicillin comes from a type of bread mold.

T F   4. Penicillin killed bacteria, but in its original form it was toxic to humans.

T F   5. Alexander Fleming extracted more than two pounds of penicillin and used it to fight diseases.

A B   6. Dr. Florey's advantages were that he had a well-equipped laboratory and a (A. brilliant assistant; B. no distractions from falling bombs).

T F   7. Dr. Fleming had kept the original penicillin growing and reproducing since he first discovered it.

T F   8. Dr. Florey succeeded in saving the life of the Oxford policeman.

T F   9. The Americans were able to mass-produce penicillin.

T F   10. Dr. Fleming was knighted for his discovery of penicillin.

T F   11. Fleming, Florey, and Chain all received a share of the Nobel Prize in medicine for their discovery.

T F   12. Penicillin is the only mold that has been found to fight infection.

T F   13. Once a wonder drug kills a type of micro-organism, it is never a threat again.

Medicine in Today's World

During the second half of the 1900s, doctors moved into two areas hardly explored before: organ transplants and artificial organs.

Doctors had attempted blood transfusions in the 1800s. These transfusions were hit or miss affairs. The process proved too dangerous to be practical. Sometimes the patients lived; often they died.

In the early 1900s, doctors learned that blood can be of four types (O, A, B, and AB) and have two factors (RH+ and RH-). Blood type is not based upon race or nationality. An Irishman can have the same blood as an American Indian, yet have blood different from that of his own relatives.

Suppose samples of blood from two individuals are mixed.

SYMPTOMS

1. Blood transfusions had proven to be too dangerous to be practical.

2. Otherwise healthy people were dying because of the failure of a single organ.

3. Doctors did not understand how diseases were passed from parent to child through heredity.

Can You Diagnose the Discoveries?

The samples will either mix completely, or, they may react with one another, forming blood clots. If the clots form inside the body, death results. Doctors learned how to tell if blood transfusions could be made successfully. They based the rules upon the blood type. Blood of type O can be donated to any individual. Blood of type AB can only be given to others with type AB.

In the United States, Dr. Charles Richard Drew, an African American, was a pioneer in using blood transfusions and in establishing blood banks. When properly stored, blood can be kept for about a month.

Like our muscles, heart, and kidneys, blood is a collection of cells with a special purpose. A blood transfusion is really the first step toward organ transplants from one individual to another.

Before 1954 no organ had ever been successfully transplanted from one human being to another. During that year, Ronald Herrick donated one of his kidneys to his identical twin brother, Richard Herrick. Normally, Richard's own defense system would have rejected the kidney as a foreign body. However, since the two young men were identical twins, their

Dr. Charles Richard Drew, an African American, was a pioneer in using blood transfusions and establishing blood banks.

organs could be transplanted without fear of rejection.

One of the most dramatic events in medicine of the 1900s took place in the operating room of Groote Schuur Hospital in Cape Town, South Africa. On December 3, 1967, Dr. Christaan Barnard transplanted a heart. The heart came from a human being who had died in an automobile accident. Dr. Barnard put it into another human being who was dying of heart disease.

The accident victim and heart patients were not related. Christaan Barnard had to overcome the problem of rejection. Rejection can be controlled, although not eliminated entirely, by special drugs. These drugs help the body tolerate foreign organs. The same drugs prevent the body from fighting disease bacteria. It's a delicate balance: keep the body from rejecting the transplanted organ, yet do not weaken the defenses so much that infection kills the patient.

Another solution for a failing organ is to replace it with an artificial one. Paul Revere made false teeth out of animal bone. Ambroise Paré made artificial legs and arms for his patients who had their own limbs amputated. Many body parts have artificial replacements.

During the 1940s Dr. Willem Kolff, working in Holland, developed the basic idea of an artificial kidney. Our kidneys are absolutely essential for removing waste products from the blood. Dr. Kolff's machine made it possible for waste products to be removed, but the blood itself to be unharmed.

Dr. Kolff took his design to the United States. There he built the first kidney machine. It was large and complex. The patient had to regularly go to the hospital for treatment. At first far more patients asked for treatment than the machines could serve. Doctors had to make the heart-rending decision about whom to treat and whom to turn away.

Devices like eyeglasses, hearing aids, and kidney machines operate outside the body. Artificial parts can be placed within the body, too. Heart pacemakers help regulate the speed at which a heart beats. Replacement parts for knees and hips are placed in the body. One goal is to make kidney machines and even artificial heart pumps that will fit inside the body.

On Dec. 3, 1967, Dr. Christian Barnard transplanted a heart from an accident victim to an unrelated patient. He had to overcome the problem of rejection by finding drugs which would help the body tolerate the new organ. This was one of the most dramatic events in medicine in the 1900s.

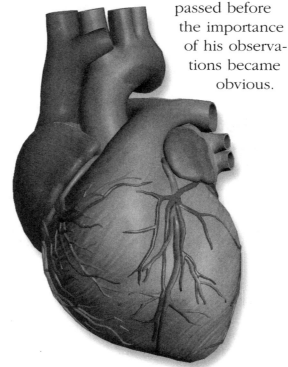

How many of the ideas described above will turn out to be breakthroughs in medicine? In many cases it is difficult to decide right away whether or not a discovery is really a breakthrough. Time must pass before we can judge the merit of a discovery.

For example, Alexander Fleming discovered penicillin in 1928, but it didn't come into common usage until the late 1940s. Leeuwenhoek first noticed bacteria in the late 1600s. Two hundred years passed before the importance of his observations became obvious.

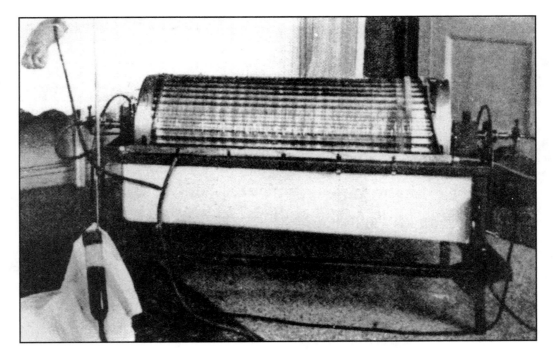

During the 1940s, Dr. Willem Kolff, working in Holland, developed the basic idea of an artificial kidney. His hemodialysis unit (right) was the first artificial organ. Our kidneys (below) are absolutely essential for removing waste products from the blood. Kolf's machine took the body's place by removing the waste products while leaving the blood itself unharmed.

Of course, a "breakthrough" may instead be a blind alley that causes more harm than good. As we have seen, doctors followed the four-humor theory of Hippocrates for 2,500 years. Yet, it and the practice of bloodletting proved to be dangerous to patients.

In the 1950s, James Watson and Francis Crick of England made a model of DNA. This double helix molecule passes traits from parents to offspring. DNA contains the genetic code that describes to the body how it is to grow. In the late 1900s, research facilities all over the world began mapping the human chromosomes. A complete map will go a long way to identifying the cause and prevention of hereditary diseases. One way that doctors can use the map is to search for ways to treat and reverse the progress of diseases such as muscular dystrophy.

Late in the 1990s, modern medicine became more aware of the importance of treating the whole person. Hippocrates said, "Illness is sometimes stronger when a mind is troubled." Ambroise Paré once built a machine that made the sound

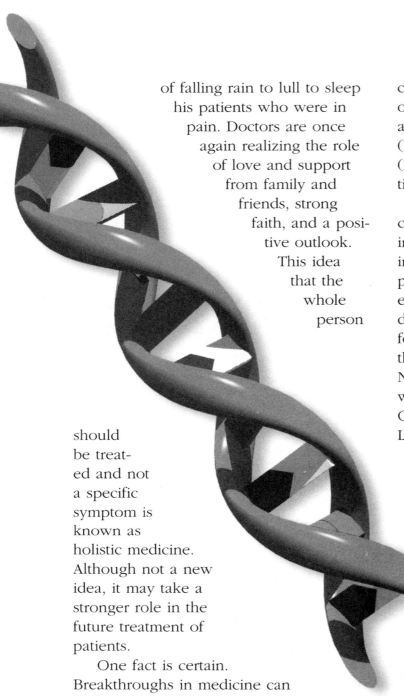

of falling rain to lull to sleep his patients who were in pain. Doctors are once again realizing the role of love and support from family and friends, strong faith, and a positive outlook. This idea that the whole person should be treated and not a specific symptom is known as holistic medicine. Although not a new idea, it may take a stronger role in the future treatment of patients.

One fact is certain. Breakthroughs in medicine can come from any direction. Look at the occupations of those whose discoveries are described in this book: janitor (Leeuwenhoek), barber (Paré), dentist (Morton), chemist (Pasteur), nuclear scientist (Roentgen) and, yes, even doctors.

This book has looked at the key discoveries of medicine. Who can resist making a list of the most important advances in medical science? Listed on the next page are the discoveries that have benefited the healing arts the most. Others may decide in favor of one event over another for this list. However, there is agreement that these advances are of the first rank. Notice that many who made discoveries were devout in their service to the Creator. Joseph Lister, Antoni Leeuwenhoek, Humphry Davy, Louis Pasteur, and many others were humble Christians.

A strand of DNA contains the genetic code that describes to the body how it is to grow and function. Every physical trait about a person can be found in this code, which is contained in nearly every cell in the human body. The field of genetic engineering is one of the fastest growing fields in medicine. Doctors are mapping the human chromosomes in the DNA code. They are manipulating genes in animals and bacteria to make them produce chemicals that humans need. Cures for several diseases have already been produced.

DIAGNOSES

1. Dr. Richard Drew established the use of transfusions and blood banks.

2. Dr. Christian Barnard performed the first heart transplant.

3. Dr. William Kolff developed an artificial kidney machine.

4. James Watson and Francis Crick discovered DNA.

Great Medical Discoveries

— Design of the human body. Andreas Vesalius published *The Fabric of the Human Body* in 1543.

— Circulation of blood. William Harvey published *On the Motion of the Blood* in 1628.

— Discovery of microscopic life. Antoni Leeuwenhoek discovered micro-organisms and glimpsed bacteria, about 1674.

— Vaccination against diseases. Edward Jenner discovered vaccination against smallpox in 1796.

— Anesthesia to kill pain during surgery. William Morton made the first public demonstration in 1846. Crawford Long had been the first to use ether in 1842. Other scientists who contributed include Humphry Davy, James Simpson, and Charles Jackson.

— Antiseptic surgery to exclude germs from the operating room, primarily developed by Joseph Lister, demonstrated in 1865.

— Germ theory of disease. Louis Pasteur had the primary role in proving that germs cause disease. His public demonstration of anthrax vaccine in 1882 established the theory against the harshest critics.

— X-rays. Wilhelm Roentgen started a second scientific revolution with the discovery of x-rays in 1895.

— Wonder drugs. Alexander Fleming found penicillium mold growing in a petri dish in 1928. From it came penicillin and other drugs that could kill bacteria without harming human cells.

— We cannot predict who will make the next breakthrough.

It could be you!

Bibliography

Asimov, Isaac. *Asimov's Biographical Encyclopedia of Science and Technology.* second revised edition. Garden City, NY: Doubleday & Company, Inc., 1982.

Asimov, Isaac. *A Short History of Biology.* Garden City: The Natural History Press, 1964.

Crook, Bette and Charles L. *Famous Firsts in Medicine.* NY: G.P. Putnam's Sons, 1974.

Dubos, Renè. *Pasteur and Modern Science.* Garden City: Doubleday & Co., Inc., 1960.

Eberle, Irmengarde. *Modern Medical Discoveries.* NY: Thomas Y. Crowell Co., 1968.

Hall, A. Rupert and Marie Boas. *A Brief History of Science.* NY: Signet Science Library, 1964.

Hart, Michael H. *The 100: A Ranking of the Most Influential Persons in History.* Secaucus, NJ: Carol Publishing Group, 1993.

Hume, Ruth Fox. *Great Men of Medicine.* NY: Random House, 1961.

Kruif, Paul D. *Microbe Hunters.* NY: Harcourt, Brace and Co., 1926.

McKenzie, A. E. E. *The Major Achievements of Science.* New York: Simon and Schuster, 1960.

Morris, Henry M. *Men of Science, Men of God.* San Diego: Creation-Life Publishers, 1982.

Poole, Lynn and Gray. *Scientists Changed the World.* NY: Dodd, Mead & Co., 1962.

Riedman, Sarah R. *Shots without Guns.* NY: Rand McNally & Co., 1960.

Shippen, Katherine B. *Men of Medicine.* NY: The Viking Press, 1957.

Silverberg, Robert. *The Great Doctors.* NY: G. P. Putnam's Sons, 1964.

Tarshis, Jerome. *Andreas Vesalius.* NY: The Dial Press, Inc., 1968.

Vallery-Radot, Rene. *The Life of Louis Pasteur.* Garden City: Doubleday & Company, 1927.

Wright, Helen and Samuel Rapport, Eds. *The Amazing World of Medicine.* NY: Harper & Brothers, 1961.

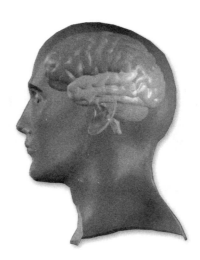

Answers to Chapter Questions

Chapter 1:
1. F
2. B
3. T
4. A
5. A
6. B
7. A
8. B
9. B
10. F
11. T

Chapter 2:
1. F
2. B
3. F
4. T
5. T
6. A
7. T
8. T

Chapter 3:
1. A
2. F
3. B
4. T
5. F
6. T
7. A
8. T
9. F
10. F
11. T
12. B
13. C
14. D
15. F
16. E
17. A

Chapter 4:
1. A
2. F
3. C
4. B
5. Love
6. D
7. God
8. F
9. B

Chapter 5:
1. B
2. T
3. B
4. A
5. pump
6. T
7. F
8. T
9. B
10. A
11. D
12. C

Chapter 6:
1. C
2. T
3. A
4. F
5. B
6. A
7. B
8. A
9. C
10. E
11. F
12. D

Chapter 7:
1. F
2. F
3. B
4. T
5. B
6. F
7. T
8. F
9. D
10. F
11. B
12. E
13. C
14. G
15. A

Chapter 8:
1. T
2. F
3. B
4. C
5. F
6. B
7. F
8. F
9. B
10. B
11. T

Chapter 9:
1. T
2. D
3. A
4. B
5. F
6. C
7. C
8. C
9. B
10. A
11. T
12. B
13. A
14. D
15. C

Chapter 10:
1. B
2. B
3. B
4. B
5. T
6. F
7. T
8. A
9. B
10. T

Chapter 11:
1. B
2. F
3. B
4. F
5. C
6. T
7. B
8. B
9. B
10. T
11. A

Chapter 12:
1. T
2. T
3. C
4. B
5. T
6. B
7. B
8. F
9. T
10. D

Chapter 13:
1. C
2. C
3. D
4. F
5. F
6. B
7. T
8. A
9. A
10. T

Chapter 14:
1. T
2. F
3. T
4. A
5. B
6. T
7. B
8. F
9. T
10. F
11. F
12. T
13. F
14. T

Chapter 15:
1. B
2. T
3. B
4. F
5. T
6. T
7. F
8. E
9. C
10. B
11. A
12. D
13. F

Chapter 16:
1. A
2. F
3. B
4. F
5. F
6. A
7. F
8. F
9. C
10. T

Chapter 17:
1. T
2. F
3. B
4. F
5. B
6. A
7. D
8. A
9. T
10. D
11. F
12. T
13. B
14. D
15. A
16. C

Chapter 18:
1. B
2. F
3. B
4. B
5. B
6. D
7. T
8. B
9. B
10. F
11. F

Chapter 19:
1. T
2. B
3. F
4. B
5. T
6. F
7. A
8. F
9. C
10. D
11. B
12. A
13. E

Chapter 20:
1. B
2. B
3. T
4. F
5. F
6. A
7. T
8. F
9. T
10. T
11. T
12. F
13. F

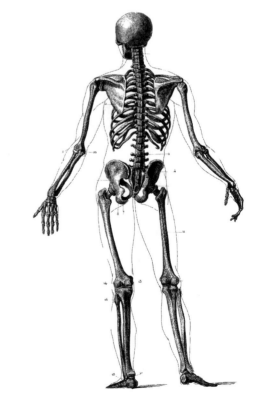

Index

Illustrations/Photo Credits

EXPLORING PLANET EARTH

JOHN HUDSON TINER

An amazing look at the history of our planet from a creationism perspective. With definition of terms and identification of famous explorers, scientists, inventions, and etc., this book gives students an excellent initial knowledge of people and places, encouraging them to continue their studies in depth. By bringing to life the explorations of people like Marco Polo and Christopher Columbus, the author gives students the opportunity to read history that hasn't been altered or erased altogether. Includes chapter review questions.

$13.99

ISBN 0-89051-178-0 • 160 pages • 8-1/2 x 11 • Paperback
Contains black and white photos and illustrations

Available at Christian bookstores nationwide
Find other great titles at www.masterbooks.net

EXPLORING THE WORLD OF CHEMISTRY

JOHN HUDSON TINER

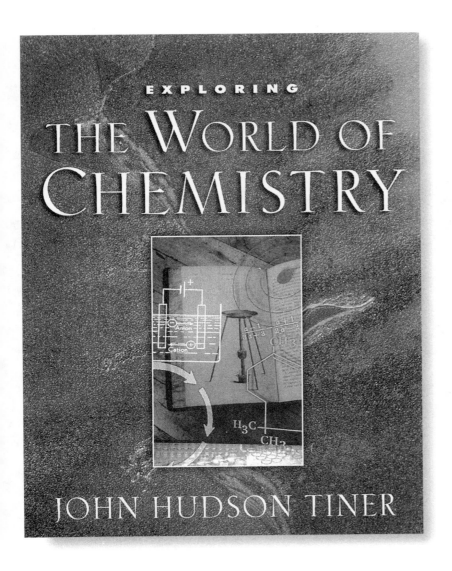

AVAILABLE FALL 2000!

From the search to make gold to the latest advances in silicon microchips, *Exploring Chemistry* takes the reader on an exciting tour of the major achievements of chemistry. Each chapter contains vivid descriptions, exciting action and stirring biographies. Chapters are packed with illustrations, end of chapter questions and a thorough index.

Advances in chemistry are described through the lives of the chemists who made the exciting discoveries. The fascinating breakthroughs in chemistry come alive, providing students with an educational and entertaining look at the discoveries of chemistry.

The chapters focus on individuals who made chemical discoveries that changed the world. Robert Boyle, John Dalton, Michael Faraday and many others were outspoken in their Christian beliefs.

The book is prepared for the homeschool market and can serve as a textbook and reading resource. Parents can share it with young children through read-aloud. Later, students can revisit the material for a more in-depth study.

$13.99

ISBN 0-89051-248-5 • 160 pages • 8-1/2 x 11 • Paperback
Contains black and white photos and illustrations

Available at Christian bookstores nationwide
Find other great titles at www.masterbooks.net

CHAMPIONS OF DISCOVERY SERIES

JOHN HUDSON TINER

Tiner, an educator and author of books like *Exploring the History of Medicine* and *Exploring Planet Earth*, uses his communication skills to introduce this new series.

In this first book, we learn that inventors like Charles Babbage (computer), Michael Faraday (electric generator), and John Gutenberg (movable type/printing press) gave credit for their achievements to God.

The *Champions of Discovery Series* lists many of the great men of science who also held to a firm faith in God. From Sir Isaac Newton to Louis Pasteur, these intellectuals merely considered that they were thinking God's thoughts after Him. Tiner, a science teacher, brings these sometimes-forgotten scientists into our consciousness and demonstrates that legitimate scientists have historically affirmed the Bible's teachings.

CHAMPIONS OF INVENTION
ISBN 0-89051-278-7

CHAMPIONS OF MATH
ISBN 0-89051-279-5

CHAMPIONS OF SCIENCE
ISBN 0-89051-280-9

$5.99

5-1/4 x 8-1/2 • PAPERBACK • 96 pages

Available at Christian bookstores nationwide
Find other great titles at www.masterbooks.net

THE ASTRONOMY BOOK

DR. JONATHAN HENRY

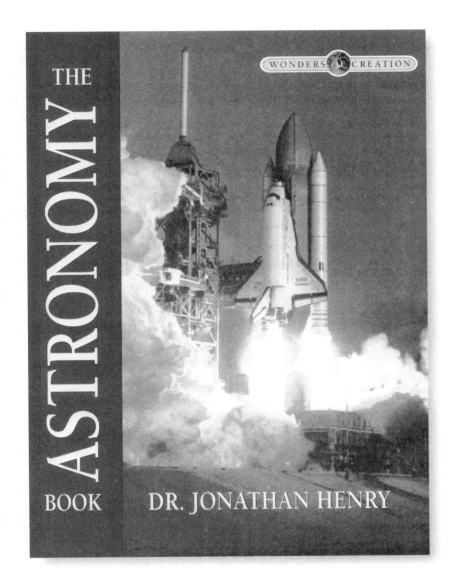

The second book in the highly successful "Wonders of Creation" series, The Astronomy Book soars through the solar system targeting middle-school through junior-high levels. The reader will acquire a wealth of knowledge on subjects such as supernovas, red shift, facts about planets, and much more. Enhanced with dozens of color photos and illustrations (including NASA shots), this book gives educators and students a Christian-based look at the awesomeness of the heavens

Abbreviated Table of Contents

$15.99

ISBN 0-89051-250-7 • 80 pages • 8-1/2 x 11 • Casebound
Four-color interior

Available at Christian bookstores nationwide
Find other great titles at www.masterbooks.net